W9-CLE-459

830

WILLIAM FAULKNER

Modern Literature Monographs

ooo

WILLIAM FAULKNER

Joachim Seyppel

Frederick Ungar Publishing Co.
New York

Published by arrangement with Colloquium Verlag, Berlin.
Translated from the original German, with revisions, by
the author.

Copyright © 1971 by Frederick Ungar Publishing Co., Inc.
Printed in the United States of America
Library of Congress Catalog Card Number: 74–134826
ISBN: 0–8044–2820–4 (cloth)
0–8044–6859–1 (paper)

ooo

A Personal
Reflection

When this book was in the making it seemed to me both entirely superfluous and absolutely necessary. Because so many voluminous studies have been written on Faulkner, professors—so I thought—might ponder why the publisher asked the author to translate his own German essay into English. The answer is simple. Just because so many scholarly volumes about a difficult author exist—making, it seemed to me, the job of appreciating Faulkner not easier but harder—a brief, concise introduction to this author is absolutely necessary. I concentrated, however, on one very important feature in Faulkner's work, somewhat neglected by scholars: the theme of the *hermaphrodite*. In this respect, this introduction to Faulkner in general became an introduction to a specialized interpretation.

The book is necessary to me in another respect. Through my occupation with Faulkner I found myself as an author. Thus the town of Hammond, Louisiana, became in some respects my own private domain—a place like that partly mythical Yoknapatawpha County that Faulkner invented for himself. In Hammond I met

Tom Maddox, giant of the local tennis courts, Clark and Liz Gallagher, giants of the local language and music departments, and all the other likable people of a small town in the Deep South. Here my daughter was born. Part of that locality was incorporated into *columbus bluejeans*, the novel later published in Germany. This essay is therefore a very personal and in this respect a necessary contribution to Faulkner and his world. I am sure, moreover, that it will call for very personal and therefore necessary responses.

                                                        J. S.

ooo

Contents

1

ooooooooooooooooooooooooooooooooooooooooooooooooo

Introduction to Certain Problems

If there be grief, then let it be but rain,
And this but silver grief for grieving's sake,
If these green woods be dreaming here to wake
Within my heart, if I should rouse again.

But I shall sleep, for where is any death
While in these blue hills slumbrous overhead
I'm rooted like a tree? Though I be dead,
This earth that holds me fast will find me breath.[1]

That an essay of this sort begins with a quotation from *A Green Bough* indicates not only that William Faulkner began his writing career as a poet, but that he remained something of a "poet"—of a dithyrambic author—up to and through his last epics. Indeed, he can probably be best understood and appreciated as a poetic writer. The Dionysian element—a mingling of heroic passion and tragedy, a state of exaltation—is the literary trait most characteristic of Faulkner, and can scarcely be found in such a pure form anywhere else in modern literature.

Dionysus or Bacchus, the god of fertility and vegetation, living in a tree or in the never withering ivy, is embodied in Melisandre Backus' father, a farmer in the late novel *The Town*, who lives "on a plantation about six miles from town" with a bottle of whiskey and who spends his time "sitting on the gallery in summer and in the library in winter with the bottle, reading Latin poetry." [2] This description also fits Faulkner himself. Another man much like the author is depicted in his first novel, *Soldiers' Pay*: the rector picks up the faunlike Januarius Jones and welcomes him with a bottle of Scotch extracted from a drawer—"A sop to the powers." [3]

The life and work of William Faulkner may be

presented as scenes in a pageant of Christ's resurrection, as in the resurrection of that Protestant rector from his neopagan surroundings. This combination of classical mythology and Christian religion may have confused and even repelled a great part of the reading public from the very beginning of Faulkner's career. America has accepted Faulkner only very hesitatingly, just as he accepted his country only with great reservations. Abroad, he has apparently been appreciated with at least as great a critical understanding as at home, especially in France (through Gide and Sartre), and in Germany (where he gained early fame through his publisher Rowohlt) he was readily deemed the greatest exponent of modern American literature.

No analysis of Faulkner's works can avoid certain difficulties in introducing the reader into the labyrinth of the Deep South in which they are set. First, the rhetorical style with its long-winded passages estranges the Anglo-Saxon reader even more than the European reader. American critics have often complained about Faulkner's style, his faults in composition, certain obscurities in plot, and the confusions that arise from the nonchronological order of his publications (after the success of *Sanctuary* old manuscripts were published by journals that had rejected them earlier). Non-American critics and especially translators have complained about the impossibility of putting into another language something that seems so entirely peculiar to the diction of the Deep South. Hemingway was, in this respect, a relatively "easy" writer to translate. Nothing illustrates better the uniqueness of Faulkner than the problems that arise with foreign editions. An American reader might be well advised to consider this aspect, because he can then observe Faulkner from a new viewpoint. The feasibility of a translation is, in one way or another, an interesting criterion of the qualities of a writer, that is, of his universality, which in Faulkner's case is, paradoxically, one of his strengths.

The title of the novel *Light in August*, for example, seems readily understandable, and is clearly a very good and appropriate title. "Light," however, is not only a substantive but an adjective, and it can be a verb. Critics have noted that "August" also means "majestic"; in this meaning the word is used twice on the first page of the short story "A Rose for Emily" ("august names"), but, of course, in the title it cannot be used in this way. "Light in August" may refer to the bearing of a child in August, that is, to Lena's child; in the Deep South the phrase "she is light" is often used to describe a woman who has given birth to a child.

"I've been told," said one questioner to Faulkner at the class conferences at the University of Virginia, "that the title of *Light in August* came from a colloquialism for the completion of a pregnancy. Is that true?" "No," Faulkner answered, "I used it because in my country in August there's a peculiar quality to light and that's what the title means. It has in a sense nothing to do with the book at all, the story at all." [4]

European critics, schooled in the tradition of Cervantes, Laurence Sterne, and Thomas Mann, were perhaps better able to appreciate Faulkner than reviewers from New York or New Orleans. Southern eloquence and the "Gothic" tradition in Faulkner were therefore hindrances to an acceptance of his work by literary circles in the United States. He once remarked that Hemingway never had enough courage to write a single word that the reader had to look up in the dictionary; Faulkner himself had this courage in excess.

Some of his words are to be found in no dictionary at all. Even if readers understand each of his words, however, they must still confront the sheer quantity of his language, the sentences and passages that cover many lines or even pages, the insertions, italics, unorthodox punctuation, overlappings, bracketings, flashbacks. Faulkner is not only a "Gothic" author, but a "baroque" one, with a tendency toward a naive form of romanticism. He is a storyteller of exuberant imagination, spontaneous—or so it seems—like a part of nature. Where the "nature" of his writing ends and where "art" begins is often an open question.

2

○○

A Lost Generation

William Faulkner belongs to that grandiose, though "lost" generation whose members were all born shortly before or at the turn of the century. It is a generation that, with John Dos Passos (born 1896), Thornton Wilder and William Faulkner (born 1897), Ernest Hemingway (born 1899), and Thomas Wolfe (born 1900), greatly dominates the international literary scene of the first half of the twentieth century. These writers have only a second-hand knowledge of the Civil War and the American frontier, of the expansion to the West, of the gold rush, Indian wars, and the settling of new land by their forefathers—but they are the products of these events. They have become used to the steamer, the automobile, even the airplane (which plays such a great role with Faulkner), to industrialization, money values, and expansion abroad. They have turned to other continents, especially Europe, from which their fathers came. They have a new way of looking at the world, formed of a nostalgia for the land that was once the "new" world, as well as of a regard for the regions that used to be the "old" world.

That "old" world, however, has a new sort of fascination for them. Their own "heroic" times—wars of independence and civil strife—take on a new meaning in reference to the last "heroic" war of worldwide dimensions, World War I. They do not write historical novels, however. When Faulkner looks back on the Civil War, he looks back on man as he is today; man changes only his costume, not his nature. When, moreover, as in *Soldiers' Pay* or *Mosquitoes*, he writes "contemporary" novels, this contemporaneousness extends backward and beyond the present moment into some form of timelessness. The contemporaneousness of man is not only, as in the work of Spengler or Toynbee, cultural and historic, but also metaphysical. The dimensions explored by the "lost generation" are those of the psyche and of symbols; the geographic dimensions, which these writers add to their native American orientation, include most of the countries of Europe.

Despite this extension of their vision, a higher standard of living, relative material security, the increasing power in world politics of their respective national administrations, and despite all "progress," these writers between 1920 and 1930 see themselves as condemned. Most probably World War I evoked their feeling of homelessness; this war constitutes the real break between the nineteenth and the twentieth centuries.

Faulkner is no exception to the rule. Born in the Deep South, he watched the Northern industries penetrate his native soil, bringing an inflation of all values that, however, does not mean inflation of happiness. On the contrary, the misery of the Deep South since "The War Between the States" only then becomes fully obvious. The antebellum period and even the Civil War therefore gain a romantic color they never before possessed: they gain greatness, heroism, and glory. America entering the World War promises new heroism, but only a deepened feeling of misery and guilt remains.

Faulkner joined the Royal Air Force in Canada but never reached Europe during the war. In the 1920's, however, he toured the battlefields of France. Such short stories as "Turnabout" were inspired by experiences of the war. After another thirty-five years he returned to the European scene of the years between 1914 and 1918; *A Fable* is the novel of the French corporal and the old marshal, who in those decisive days of the dawn of the twentieth century

confront one another symbolically. Faulkner's last trip
to the Old World took place when he was awarded
the Nobel Prize for Literature. Even in his later works,
such as *The Town* or *The Mansion,* several reminis-
cences of Europe appear: in episodes that take place in
Germany and that are rather Franco- than Germano-
phile he settles up with the "new" Germans.

One of the major differences between Faulkner
and other great writers of the lost generation is that he
was a true product of the peculiarities of the Deep
South. Hemingway's writings show relatively little
evidence of the North, of Illinois, where he was born;
Thornton Wilder more or less assumed the role of a
world citizen; Dos Passos became the critic of contemporary industrial society in general and of American society in particular. Only Thomas Wolfe, another
Southerner, suggests the unique atmosphere that is also
Faulkner's principal source of inspiration. Race prejudice, heightened by the passions of the subtropics and
deepened by the dubious religiosity of the Bible Belt,
prevails throughout. Such motives as incest, murder,
lynching, the shadowy world of a human and at the
same time beastly jungle, spread in Faulkner's work.
Mississippi, the state and the river, New Orleans and
the Gulf of Mexico, the swamps and the sunburnt
fields are his scenes: a world as much a chaos as a
cosmos. Somewhere in the heart of this world lies
mythical Jefferson in Yoknapatawpha County, which
in some of Faulkner's books is even shown in a detailed
map.

One week after he was informed of being awarded the Nobel Prize for Literature, Faulkner, according
to various reports, went with his friends on the usual
annual hunt, got hopelessly drunk in keeping with
the old tradition, and then lay in bed half unconscious

for several days. He came to only shortly before the flight for Sweden, and, pale and weakened, he made the trip. In Stockholm, however, he made a profound impression through his distinguished appearance and through his acceptance speech, which contained the following memorable passage:

Our tragedy today is a general and universal physical fear so long sustained by now that we can even bear it. There are no longer problems of the spirit. There is only the question: When will I be blown up? Because of this, the young man or woman writing today has forgotten the problem of the human heart in conflict with itself which alone can make good writing because only that is worth writing about, worth the agony and the sweat. He must learn them again. He must teach himself that the basest of all things is to be afraid; and, teaching himself that, forget it for ever, leaving no room in his workshop for anything but the old verities and truths of the heart, the old universal truths lacking which any story is ephemeral and doomed—love and honour and pity and pride and compassion and sacrifice. Until he does so, he labours under a curse. He writes not of love but of lust, of defeats in which nobody loses anything of value, of victories without hope and, worst of all, without pity or compassion. His griefs grieve on no universal bones, leaving no scars. He writes not of the heart but of the glands. Until he relearns these things, he will write as though he stood among and watched the end of man. I decline to accept the end of man. It is easy enough to say that man is immortal simply because he will endure: that when the last ding-dong of doom has clanged and faded from the last worthless rock hanging tideless in the last red and dying evening, that even then there will still be one more sound: that of his puny, inexhaustible voice, still talking. I refuse to accept this. I believe that man will not merely endure: he will prevail. He is immortal, not because he alone among creatures has an inexhaustible voice, but because he has a soul, a spirit capable of compassion and sacrifice and endurance. The poet's, the writer's, duty is to write about these things.[1]

This is the complete, the paradoxical Faulkner, with all his weaknesses and strengths. The speech indicates a literary program that he often enough abandoned; because he has written, apparently, more often about human behavior as the result of glandular processes than about the human heart. Orgy and humanism, ecstasy and insight are his antithetical motifs. Why, after all, should a writer have a program? Faulkner is above all a spontaneous storyteller, a man of fiction in its truest and somewhat old-fashioned meaning—an author who saw a new literary style or theory like that of James Joyce come just at the right moment to help him make a virtue out of the vice of wordiness.

The knack for spinning a yarn ran in his family. In the Deep South the tradition of talking and listening is still honored, and a bad speech there is still worth more than a good piece of writing. Faulkner's persons just love to tell stories, to any listener at all. Faulkner's great-grandfather was the author of the sentimental novel *The White Rose of Memphis*, published in 1880; it sold 160,000 copies in thirty-five printings. Young Will Falkner, as he used to spell his name, was certainly influenced in his decisions by his great-grandfather's literary success.

Faulkner was born at New Albany, Mississippi, on September 25, 1897. Later he lived some thirty miles away, in Oxford. He was an average student, always ready for mischief, full of imagination and determined quite early in life to become a writer like his great-grandfather. He never had any difficulty in relating a story. While he talked, his schoolmates would do his homework for him. Fantasy and reality, fiction and truth have since become a strange unity in his work, as have the spheres of past and present which, in the Deep South, have never quite been kept distinct. Here unreality has a form of existence that elsewhere would be described as "mentally unbalanced."

As a youth Faulkner began to write verse. He grew increasingly estranged from the world of his schoolmates and from sports, and he did not even finish high school. He read much and hectically, if aimlessly. Roamed the woods. Stayed alone. A good-for-nothing from Mississippi. A young fellow from the nearby world of Tom Sawyer and Huckleberry Finn.

A friend of young Faulkner, Phil Stone, who was a witness to the vagabond's first attempt at writing, later influenced his career decisively, from the literary point of view as well as from the material. Stone introduced him to Shakespeare, Swinburne, Keats, Shelley, Dickens, Conrad, to the great French writers Balzac and Flaubert, and finally to James Joyce. He also led Faulkner, in 1918, to enter the Royal Air Force in Canada.

In the early 1920's, Faulkner began to write short stories and to submit them to publishers. Unsuccessful as a writer, he earned a living at various jobs. He did not need much for his unorthodox way of life, living at home and keeping expenses at a minimum. As a guest student at the University of Mississippi he broadened his education, especially in Romance literature; he failed an English course, however, and thereupon left the academic world. Again he took up his irregular life. In the mask of a vagabonding Southern farmer the future writer slowly evolved.

Not surprisingly, the citizens of Oxford regarded the outsider with deep distrust. Faulkner, however, cared little for the opinions of his neighbors. He became increasingly introspective, had doubts about his literary talents, but nevertheless continued to write. A sojourn in New York led nowhere. He was offered the position of postmaster in Oxford, accepted, but made a mess of it, and finally gave up after public protests. He was, he said, no longer exposed to every "son of a bitch" who happened to have two cents for a stamp.

As postmaster, he had time to write poems. They were published in Boston by The Four Seas Company under the title *The Marble Faun*, in a private edition made possible by his friend Phil Stone. The poems were poorly received in the circles for which they had been written, and only a few copies were sold. In New Orleans, Faulkner met one of the trailblazers of modern American literature, Sherwood Anderson. The meeting later led to the publication of Faulkner's first novel, *Soldiers' Pay*. Faulkner's appearance and way of life in those years may be seen in his next book, *Mosquitoes*, in a description that a girl gives of a "funny man," a "little kind of black man." "A nigger?" asks her girlfriend.

No. He was a white man, except he was awful sunburned and kind of shabby dressed—no necktie and hat. Say, he said some funny things to me. . . . He said he was a liar by profession. . . . I think he was crazy. Not dangerous: just crazy.

The question of his name arises:

Walker or Foster or something. . . . It must be Foster because I remembered it by it began with a F like my girlfriend's middle name. . . . Only I don't think it was Foster, because . . . Oh, yes: I remember—Faulkner, that was it.[2]

Faulkner remained this professional "liar" for the rest of his life, inventing the most improbable stories, like the one in which sheep become fish and the shepherd becomes a shark. The hint by the girl in *Mosquitoes* that the "little dark one" could possibly be a Negro turned into a significant motif in one of Faulkner's greatest novels, *Light in August*. In this book, Joe Christmas is never accepted by white or black, and until his death he searches for his individual identity as a human being.

Before Faulkner's first novels were published, he repeatedly attempted to write conservative short stories. The *Times-Picayune* in New Orleans has the distinction of being the first to have published one of them. Faulkner's development as an author was extremely slow. He deliberately took his time. He oriented himself to authors whom he personally met in New Orleans, like Sandburg and Sinclair Lewis, Oliver La Farge and Hamilton Basso. In the mid-1920's he went on a European spree. When he returned, after about one year, *Soldiers' Pay* had been published. In 1927, *Mosquitoes* appeared. These books resulted in practically nothing and brought him neither literary success nor royalties. The publisher canceled his contract, which had called for three manuscripts. Thus, after half a decade of intense work as a writer, Faulkner stood again where he had begun. He was thirty years old and had achieved as good as nothing.

Faulkner did not give up. He began another novel, *Sartoris*, which he finished in 1927. He attempted to suit the public taste and to make certain compromises with the reading public. The manuscript was accepted, but remained unpublished in a New York safe.

Phil Stone then intervened with decisive advice. The advice was as simple as it was radical. Faulkner should not write for the larger reading public but for himself. Instead of thinking of money, critics, publishers, and fame he should concentrate on his work alone. The result of that advice was *The Sound and the Fury* (1929), perhaps Faulkner's greatest, in any case his most personal and purest achievement. It is, at the same time, the book that confronts the reader with sometimes almost insurmountable difficulties. After *Sartoris* was published in 1929, *The Sound and the Fury* followed. The former was a failure, but the latter was a *succès d'estime*. Faulkner himself, however, quite. rightly recommended *Sartoris* as the novel that people should read first, because it "has the germ of my apocrypha in it." [3]

In 1929 Faulkner married. His decision to do so may have been based on the new self-confidence that he had gained after his first literary success. Work on his next book proceeded well. In 1930 *As I Lay Dying* was published; in its overall conception it was similar to the preceding volume. Like *The Sound and the Fury*, the new piece of prose was a literary, but not a financial success. In those years Faulkner's intention to give his career a radical turn became more and more obvious; again he thought of economic stability. In this mood he wrote *Sanctuary*, the novel with the "cheap idea," as he said himself in the introduction of 1932; it was "deliberately conceived to make money." [4] The book, published in 1931, was indeed a sensation. It sold extremely well. Editors of journals soon sought Faulkner out, and even Hollywood made certain offers. Faulkner was then in a position to buy a beautiful, aristocratic antebellum mansion. Such a mansion has often played a role in the Deep South and in particular in Faulkner's work; in *Absalom, Absalom!* a mansion almost ruins its architect. Faulkner, too, needed a long time to restore his house; he needed it, as he thought, in order to feel the atmosphere of the Old South while writing.

In *The Mansion*, published in 1959, a scene toward the end demonstrates the significance of such a building for Faulkner and his region. "And now all that's left of it is a bedrode old lady and her retired old-maid schoolteacher daughter that would a lived happily ever after in sunny golden California," says Ratliff:

"But now they got to come all the way back to Missippi and live in that-ere big white elephant of a house where likely Miss Allison will have to go back to work again, maybe might even have to hump and hustle some to keep it up since how can they have mere friends and acquaintances, let alone strangers, saying how a Missippi-born and -bred lady refused to accept a whole house not only gift-free-for-nothing but that was actively theirn anyhow to begin with, without owing even Much obliged to nobody for getting it back. So maybe there's even a moral in it somewhere, if you jest knowed where to look."

The "moral" is that a house is more than just a place to live in: "even back when they said man lived in caves," Faulkner continues on the last page of the novel:

he would raise up a bank of dirt to at least keep him that far off the ground while he slept, until he invented wood floors to protect him and at last beds too, raising the floors storey by storey until they would be laying a hundred and even a thousand feet up in the air to be safe from the earth.[5]

Such a "mansion," then, lies in the center of mythical Yoknapatawpha County, the name of which derived from the Yocnany River, which was formerly called "Yocanapatafa"; Jefferson is the capital of the county. From his own mansion Faulkner could pursue his goals in relative peace. With a rare literary fertility the great novels and short stories followed one another, comprising twenty-six volumes of fiction in thirty-

eight years from 1924 (*The Marble Faun*) to 1962
(*The Reivers*)—a book every eighteen months or so.
In fact, in some years a work by Faulkner appeared
twice on the annual publishing list, and only one relatively larger gap occurs between two books: between
1942 and 1948 (not counted here are three publications; two were only slim volumes of one short story
each—"Idyll in the Desert" and "Miss Zilphia Gant"—
and "Notes on a Horsethief," which later became part
of *A Fable*). Above all, *Light in August* (1932), then
Absalom, Absalom! (1936), *The Hamlet* (1940), *Intruder in the Dust* (1948), and eventually *A Fable*
(1954) made William Faulkner known to the literary
world beyond national borders and, finally, the cycle
that began with *The Hamlet* continued with the broad
epics *The Town* (1957) and *The Mansion* (1959).

An indication of the international fame and repu-
tation of Faulkner's style and of his human and literary
character occurred when a group of Soviet Russian
writers touring the United States showed interest in
William Faulkner above all other writers. Their
aesthetic philosophy of literature, known as "socialist
realism," was broader than expected, and they found
in Faulkner the personality they had most avidly
sought.

Faulkner had two children: a son and the
daughter Jill to whom *A Fable* is dedicated. In Oxford
he spent his time with dogs, horses, hunting, farming,
and working around the house. He would only write,
as he said, when he felt like it. He died on July 6, 1962.
His death apparently made little impact on the community in which he had lived and which he had made
world famous. Only a few "of the shoppers standing in
the blazing sun on the sidewalks turned to watch as the
procession rolled past." [6]

3

ooooooooooooooooooooooooooooooooooooooooooo

The
Hermaphrodite

About the middle of Faulkner's career as a writer, around 1940, the population of the Deep South consisted of approximately one Negro to every two whites. Faulkner's home state of Mississippi, however, had 1,074,578 Negroes and 1,106,327 whites—a nearly one-to-one ratio. This numerical equality is, as we know, a fact that whites in Mississippi carry constantly and suspiciously in their mind, consciously or subconsciously. The Southern Negro seems to have become better acclimatized than the white, or perhaps was always better so since the beginning of his slavery. His fertility, the ever growing birthrate is, apparently, the phenomenon most feared by white citizenry. Because of his former low standing during the time of outright slavery the Negro has, of course, profited most in technological, economical, and cultural terms since the days of the Civil War—a form of "progress" the highest point of which is still far below the average standard of the white population in the United States.

Although part of the white population that formerly led an aristocratic life has become impoverished and is socially degraded (a fact with which one half of Faulkner's work deals), another group of whites—those who were formerly poor—has "arrived" at new wealth (a fact with which the other half of Faulkner's work deals). The Compsons are pitted against the Snopeses, and between them is "the nigger." Love and hate, race compromises and race prejudice, incest and lynching dominate the scene. To read Faulkner means to get used to sex murder, rape, abortion, impotence, ecstasy, sober brutality and intoxication, human tornados, psychic hurricanes, vampires.

The reader of Faulkner should bear in mind such topographical details as that the average temperature in the state of Mississippi is about 65°, with a subtropical humidity as an aggravating climatic factor. The average temperature at noon on a summer day in Mississippi is around 90°, and the summers are long. Human sweat has, as it were, penetrated the soil. Malaria, typhoid, yellow fever kept the life span short and the birthrates low. The mosquito, the basis of the title of one of Faulkner's novels, still reigns a good part of the day and night.

The Southern states have, to be sure, a unique literary tradition, but Faulkner seems to be the first moralist among its many storytellers—a writer who raised both moralism and storytelling to the highest level ever achieved south of the Mason-Dixon line. He knows that the problem of race relations in particular must be solved. How difficult life is in the South, how utterly uncertain the future, how problematic certain reforms, can be seen by those figures who, like Quentin Compson in *The Sound and the Fury*, commit suicide:

who loved death above all, who loved only death, loved and lived in a deliberate and almost perverted anticipation of death as a lover loves and deliberately refrains from the waiting willing friendly tender incredible body of his beloved, until he can no longer bear not the refraining but the restraint and so flings, hurls himself, relinquishing, drowning.[1]

Faulkner finds no such cheap consolation as is offered at the end of *Gone With the Wind* in the remark that "tomorrow is another day." No battle, to Faulkner, is ever won. The battle may not even be carried out. The battlefield presents itself only as the mirror of man's foolishness and despair, and victory only as an illusion of philosophers and fools.

From the subtropical, swampy, bloody soil of the

Deep South Donald Mahon goes on to the insanity of the world war; he returns with a damaged brain. This is the motif of the first novel, *Soldiers' Pay* (1926), which, from an artistic point of view, is quite imperfect. Around the scarred and almost blinded flier a group of old friends and relatives and new acquaintances gather in a small town in Georgia during a hot, humid spring; they meet in the house of the Protestant parson Mahon, Donald's father. Joe Gilligan, war comrade and nurse, falls in love with Mrs. Powers, a widow, who sees the invalid Donald on the train and decides to help bring him home; she finally marries Donald and is widowed a second time. Cecily refuses to marry the returning Donald, her fiancé before the war, and gives herself to George Farr, a simpleminded young man; she runs off with him without really finding an emotional tie. The housekeeper Emmy, who was once seduced by Donald, and Jones, the Pan-like creature, are the most contrasting couple of the novel, but they, too, like all the others, have no contact with each other.

The fathers of Donald and Cecily are portrayed most successfully although these figures hardly influence the plot. The other characters remain shadowy, pale, and imcompletely sketched. The Negroes are still only extras in the cast of the novel. Only the colored porter on the train already has something of the pride and the stubbornness of a Lucas Beauchamp from the later novel *Intruder in the Dust*; through his mere presence he shows something of the power of resistance of the Negro, of his undercurrent role. He appears as one of those, who, unobtrusively, regulate certain streams of life.

Faulkner's technique in this early attempt already deviates quite strongly and quite typically from novels of similar intent by other authors. He circumvents his plot instead of following it up in the common, traditional narrative way. He draws several biographical sketches and depicts different environments, approaches the passive "hero" only once in a close-up and tells, in subsequent passages, of his being shot down and wounded, covering his death at the same time. Faulkner's "hero" is only a pretext for the analysis of other people's fates. Donald Mahon as the center of little importance directs our attention to more significant circles of life around him.

Through certain experiments with the stream-of-consciousness monologue, which is usually set in brackets, Faulkner attempts to penetrate the psychological makeup of his figures. His inexperience, however, is easily detected; he uses a literary method that had been developed only a few years earlier by James Joyce but that had already come to a sudden dead end. The novel abounds with superflouous metaphors, odd constructions, from which we may collect a dictionary of hackneyed comparisons. One example is: "and the branches of trees were as motionless as coral fathoms deep under seas. A tree frog took up his monotonous trilling and the west was a vast green lake, still as eternity." Other like phrases are: "sliced like a cheese"; "vain as a girl"; "fireflies were like lazily blown sparks"; "Jones, like a fat satyr"; "eyes, clear and yellow, obscene and old in sin as a goat's." These sequences reveal the frustrated poet.

In this novel the criticism of the American society is strong, although somewhat superficial. The Reverend Mahon says:

"And that is already the curse of our civilization. Things, Possessions, to which we are slaves, which require us to either labor honestly at least eight hours a day or do something illegal so as to keep them painted or dressed in the latest mode or filled with whisky or gasoline." [2]

Allusions to the American vamp-type come through. Faulkner's idea—or ideal—of womanhood, whether admittedly or not, seems strangely influenced by an environment in which Hollywood and smart, slick New York magazines have set certain standards of taste and judgment, and the flapper-type dominates even the small town. The automobile (as Faulkner later says in *Intruder in the Dust*) has accordingly become "our national sex symbol." The American, Faulkner says:

loves nothing but his automobile. . . . We cannot really enjoy anything unless we can go up an alley for it. Yet our whole background and raising and training forbids the sub-rosa and surreptitious. So we have to divorce our wife today in order to remove from our mistress the odium of mistress in order to divorce our wife tomorrow in order to remove from our mistress and so on. As a result of which the American woman has become cold and undersexed: she has projected her libido onto the automobile not only because its glitter and gadgets and mobility pander to her vanity and incapacity (because of the dress decreed upon her by the national retailers association) to walk but because it will not maul her and tousle her, get her all sweaty and disarranged. [3]

Vamp and frigidity—this is a synthesis that, in *Soldiers' Pay*, seems embodied in Cecily. Mrs. Powers also flaunts such a combination, but in another way. Emmy is its victim. All female persons of the novel appear, in the final analysis, to be barren.

Faulkner found the symbol for such infertility in Greek mythology, in the *hermaphrodite*. The hermaphrodite, by definition, combines the characteristics of both sexes; Faulkner's girls (or pseudo-girls) represent, as it were, the nonfunctional hermaphrodite in that only one part is really functional physically, biologically, and sexually—the female part, but in a "sexless" or frigid way.

The Hermaphroditus of Greek mythology is the son of Hermes and Aphrodite, of whom the nymph of the fountain of Salmacis in Caria became enamored; when he bathed in her fountain, she entreated the gods that she might be forever united with him, and the result was the formation of a being half man, half woman. To Sigmund Freud a "certain degree of anatomical hermaphroditism belongs to the norm"—psychic hermaphroditism means that parallel to the female inversion of the sexual object, a transformation of female psychic traits, drives, and character features into the corresponding male counterparts takes place.[4] This is hardly ever true of males.

In literature the hermaphrodite can be taken as a symbol. Michael Millgate in his extensive study *The Achievement of William Faulkner* points out that "Two important influences at this time would seem to have been Oscar Wilde and George Moore" and that it may also be "interesting to compare Faulkner's sonnet 'Hermaphroditus,' first published in *Mosquitoes*, page 252, with the lines about Salmacis in the twenty-first stanza of Wilde's poem 'The Burden of Itys.' "[5]

The step from *Soldiers' Pay* to *Mosquitoes* was, in this respect, certainly indicative. Cecily, in *Soldiers' Pay*, displays a mixture of female and male features, of boyish and girlish traits, and she is both cool and sexually attractive; as she herself admits, despite her youth she is already tired of men. The girls in the United States "don't like" the things that American soldiers learned from French women; Cecily is expressly called a hermaphrodite and therefore cannot be loved.

"This was the day of the Boy," says Faulkner in the beginning of Section Ten, Chapter Five, "Male and Female." This is a hint that for Faulkner men, too, display hermaphroditic features. Generally, however, the men in this novel seem relatively natural, although none are exactly "heroes." Januarius Jones, for example, is the fat, inhibited faun. Joe Gilligan, like most other men of the book, appears as a psychologically broken creature. Both sexes, indeed, move away from each other like particles of matter after the explosion of a harmonious universe in which Eros had been intact. A number of frightening complexes, apparently stemming from the world of Strindberg's hatred between the sexes, live on in the terrible frustrations of young people in the Deep South.

The almost total lack of any "normal" sex relations in Faulkner's work can be observed easily; this complex of utter frustration, however, may be only one of the characteristic features of modern American literature and not limited to Faulkner's Yoknapatawpha County. Neither Hemingway nor John Dos Passos, neither John Steinbeck nor Faulkner paint an American erotic idyll or know of experiences common to love stories in the European tradition (unless Europeans or Mexicans, such as those in Steinbeck's *Tortilla Flat*, are portrayed); American authors were more obsessed with "sex," and the more the mass media misused the term "love" in songs and advertisements and the like, the greater the impetus away from love and toward pure sex. The writer, said Faulkner accusingly, writes not of the heart but of the glands, and this seems especially true in his own novel *Soldiers' Pay* with its hermaphroditic figures.

A year after *Soldiers' Pay* Faulkner indirectly gives further evidence of his preoccupation with such figures in *Mosquitoes*. Here he says of his juvenile girl heroes Patricia and Jenny that each had a pelvis which could belong to a boy of fifteen; here he is fascinated by the cool and perverted sexuality of young people. Here we find the poem "Hermaphroditus" and the commentary: "A kind of sterile race: women too masculine to conceive, men too feminine to beget." [6] This dictum seems aimed not only at the persons of the novel but at the whole generation. Faulkner, in the end, accepted this form of the American dilemma; Hemingway, however, fled it, and his great mistresses come from England, Italy, or Spain.

Contrary to general opinion, *Mosquitoes* is less a psychological or sociological critique of the artist's colony of New Orleans and its snobbish admirers than a reflective and reflecting discussion on problems of aesthetics. The numerous dialogues on that theme, part ironic, part serious, tend to prove this judgment. Faulkner's own grappling with aesthetic problems takes place at an important junction of his development; it should be borne in mind that only two years later the experimental though masterly short novels *As I Lay Dying* and *The Sound and the Fury* were composed.

After his initial attempts at writing, Faulkner seemed to need some time outside rural Mississippi and some contact with fellow writers in order to clarify, theoretically, the inevitable direction of his aesthetic development. As a writer he obviously lacked certain experiences, an intellectual foundation, some literary provocations and stimuli, and a certain degree of technical ability. In New Orleans perhaps he could acquire this. New Orleans, after all, was along with New

York and San Francisco one of the three "story-cities" of the new world. Exactly to what degree Faulkner succeeded in progressing in intellectuality and technique, however, can scarcely be gathered from *Mosquitoes*; the novel rather represents a backward step in his artistic development. Its occasional humor and sarcasm and a certain verve in composition cannot conceal its utter conventionality.

A yacht party arranged by a millionairess for the bohemians of New Orleans brings a group of artists, snobs, and good-for-nothings together. Patricia stands out as the most interesting type in the group: a young girl who, as described conventionally in the framework of the novel, attempts to find some meaning in love. Her search fails; she is a hermaphrodite. The plot of the novel reveals little. It contains much small talk; a drinking bout, a swimming party, an unsuccessful flight are only pretexts for the dialogue, which skirts the subject of art. How uncertain of himself Faulkner the poet-novelist still was can be learned from the discussion of the hermaphrodite poem. "Hermaphroditus," says Fairchild:

"That's what it's about. It's a kind of dark perversion. Like a fire that don't need any fuel, that lives on its own heat. I mean, all modern verse is a kind of perversion. Like the day for healthy poetry is over and done with, that modern people were not born to write poetry any more. Other things, I grant. But not poetry. Kind of like men nowadays are not masculine and lusty enough to tamper with something that borders so close to the unnatural. A kind of sterile race: women too masculine to conceive, men too feminine to beget. . . ." [7]

Certain persons that Faulkner met in New Orleans are keys to characters in the novel; Fairchild, for example, stands for Sherwood Anderson. Although we

can identify most of the persons biographically, however, we cannot identify them artistically; they remain
real-life people without literary or symbolic significance. At best they serve as photographs of characters
of their time and day. Significantly, however, the persons whom we *cannot* identify, the girls, are more or
less typical figures from Faulkner's own repertory.

Again we are confronted with two females who
seem quite familiar to readers of *Soldiers' Pay*. Patricia,
the millionaire's niece, is a superficially cool, but deep
within herself a passionate girl (and corresponds to
Cecily in *Soldiers' Pay*); she is immature, but certainly
desirable, like unripe fruit for little boys (and the men
definitely behave like little boys). Jenny, the counter-
type, looks sensual, but displays in fact not much interest in sex, being heavy or dull (a parallel to Emmy).
As in Faulkner's first novel, the two girls together
make up one complete female person.

Significantly, the scene in which Jenny and
Patricia approach each other begins with the one
seeing the other first in the mirror. While Jenny looks
at herself in the mirror, Patricia says, "You've got a
funny figure." " 'Funny'? repeated Jenny . . . 'It's no
funnier than yours. At least my legs don't look like
birds' legs.' " When they are lying next to each other:

Jenny moved again, turning against the other's side, breath-
ing ineffably across the niece's face. The niece lay with
Jenny's passive nakedness against her arm, and moving
her arm outward from the elbow she slowly stroked the
back of her hand along the swell of Jenny's flank. Slowly,
back and forth, while Jenny lay supine and receptive as a
cat. Slowly, back and forth and back. . . . "I like flesh," the
niece murmured. "Warm and smooth. Wish I'd lived in
Rome . . . oiled gladiators . . . Jenny," she said abruptly,
"are you a virgin?" [8]

Faulkner here describes a somewhat rudimentary les-
bian scene, certainly not for its own effect but in
order to demonstrate, physically, that full female
maturity comprises Patricia's slim cool chastity as well
as Jenny's voluptuous sensuality. These two white
girls show a strong contrast to the Negro women who
figure in later works of Faulkner (like Nancy in
Requiem for a Nun) and in whom sexuality and sensuality exist in unity and natural harmony.

As for white people, Faulkner often sees himself
compelled to sketch *two* people in order to arrive at
sensuous perfection. We find such a pair in *The Wild
Palms*, which is, significantly, a double novel; it con-
sists of two stories woven together—"The Wild Palms"
and "Old Man." In one story, the farmer's wife bears a
child despite all the disaster around her; in the other
the city woman fails to bear a child despite all her
social security. A similar pair are depicted in *Light in
August* with Lena and Miss Burden.

As to the rest of *Mosquitoes*, the yacht parties
reign. Faulkner relies heavily on such clichés of Southern local color as swamps, climate, the landscape around
New Orleans, Pontchartrain Lake, and flora and fauna
of "romantically" subtropical character. The effects,
however, of the constant vexations of nature, of man's
Darwinian inferiority in the jungle, and of the fear of
malaria and typhoid, lead the characters to seek relief
in drinking.

If *Soldiers' Pay* begins with drinking, *Mosquitoes*
is one single drinking bout. Alcohol, to Faulkner,
seems to be something of a force of nature like mosquitoes, Negroes, Christianity, and the Ku Klux Klan;
in any case, it functions as substitute for another force
of nature—sex. Where even alcohol fails to carry the
plot forward, the theme of the hermaphrodite—the

unnatural in nature—is used to bring the story to a conclusion. The hermaphrodite claims a central position in Faulkner's thinking, as we shall see, and continues to appear prominently in important novels like *Sanctuary* or in great novels like *A Fable*.

To Sherwood Anderson, something like a focus of *Mosquitoes*, Faulkner dedicated his next undertaking, *Sartoris*, with the comment that through Anderson's "kindness I was first published, with the belief that this book will give him no reason to regret that fact." This third work of prose fiction is indeed a decisive step toward the final Faulkner. He plays on the main theme of the later years authoritatively: the Deep South from the Civil War to World War I, the deterioration of its old families and the ascent of new ones.

The death of four generations of the Sartoris family are portrayed. The first Sartoris is shot from behind by a Yankee, and the last is killed in a plane crash (like Faulkner's brother Dean; or like Donald Mahon, mutilated by a plane). The second Sartoris suffers a heart attack when his greatgrandson drives the car into a ditch. The third Sartoris lives just long enough to father twins who fail because of the war. Thus the machine, the new technological age (planes, cars, guns) enters even the Deep South at last.

In his way the Yankee introduced the machine and the new age into the South like a Trojan Horse bearing, in the end, only disaster and decline. Noble aristocratic Bayard Sartoris, the test pilot, victim of his guilt complex, sacrifices his life as if in atonement for the guilt of a technological mass civilization. The graves alone remain; but, "no Sartoris man to invent bombast to put on" them. "Can't even lie dead in the ground without strutting and swaggering." On the last tombstone can be read only "Bayard Sartoris. March 16, 1893—June 11, 1920."

The stone of the old Colonel, however, was different: "He stood on a stone pedestal, in his frock coat and bareheaded, one leg slightly advanced and one hand resting lightly on the stone pylon beside him." One reads:

Colonel John Sartoris, C.S.A. 1823–1876. Soldier, Statesman, Citizen of the World. For man's enlightenment he lived, By man's ingratitude he died. Pause here, son of sorrow; re-member death.[9]

This combination of Greek rhetoric, Roman grandezza, and American ideology throws an ironic and melancholy final light on the life and death of a family of the Deep South. Almost as if writing a last and crowning book, Faulkner, sad and skeptical, but just over thirty years old, has here composed the broad saga of a succession of familiar generations. From his diction, however, we may safely gather that much posing appeared in this novel. The writer seems far from sincerity and frankness. *Weltschmerz* is here, in the manner of Byron, but it is a studied attitude. Ten years later Faulkner will again pick up the story of Col-onel Sartoris, in *The Unvanquished* (apart from its re-appearance time and again in episodes and hints). *The Unvanquished*, too, has no final artistic shape; melan-choly has become grotesqueness, and neither attitude fits an author who wishes to immortalize a hero return-ing from the war.

Then the women. Narcissa—her adjective is "serene"—reminds us again of her female predecessors and like them she is very much in love with her own image; we don't need her name to realize that. She has gone some way from pure self-reflection, however,

and also from hermaphroditic behavior, foreshadow-
ing her antitype, the archetype of the earthly woman
Lena in *Light in August* when, in the end, she has a
son. He is named John. But, asks Miss Jenny, "Do you
think you can change one of 'em with a name?"

To call Faulkner's women "rather superficial," as
Irving Malin does in his interpretation,[10] because they
remain only "fanciful creations of a man who cannot
grant them emotional completeness but limits them to
extreme, willful, and isolated desires," is to misunderstand completely their meaningfully portrayed onesid-
edness. Whether hermaphrodite or womanly archetype, they are seen as full and *complete* human figures,
perfect in themselves however imperfect they may
appear to the modern eye accustomed to an entirety
that is achieved only through artificiality, fashion, or
deception.

4

ooooooooooooooooooooooooooooooooooooooooooooooo

Poetic

Experiments

In all of Faulkner's early works, the lavish use of metaphor can be observed easily. His tendency toward poetic description is reasserted throughout his career. Perhaps in order to restrain himself, in *Mosquitoes* Faulkner made a "poet" the object of his ridicule. This ridicule begins wih the poet being described as "forgotten"; his chair is vacant at lunch and the "ghostly poet" is still on the upper deck. "I wondered," says Mark, the poet, "how long it would be before some one saw fit to notify me that lunch was ready." Mark's "cold dignity" contrasts strongly with the irony of Fairchild, who remarks, "Here's a man to take your first bottle. Tell him about your scheme." Mr. Talliaferro looks at Mark and explains his "salts." "All Americans are constipated," he says.[1] Poets, then, as guinea pigs for an elixir—this is the bitter culmination of satire on a profession that is, or seems, utterly outdated.

Perhaps Faulkner thought of himself as a man to be laughed at on this occasion. *Mosquitoes* was published three years after *The Marble Faun*, that first collection of poems (dedicated "To my mother"), which "are primarily the poems of youth and a simple heart," as Phil Stone said in his preface. Faulkner took himself seriously, however, and as late as 1933 he published his second volume of verse, *A Green Bough*. The satirical comments on Mark Frost are directed only at a would-be artist; in a larger sense, they were aimed at the purely intellectual makers of verse, from whom Faulkner excluded himself.

In his literary apprenticeship Faulkner preferred the English Romantic and Victorian poets, Shelley, Tennyson, Swinburne, and the great Elizabethan authors. He began to write verse with traditional rhymes. This poetry drew Phil Stone's attention to the

young author. A European critic has noted that
Faulkner writes something like metaphorical abbrevia-
tions of certain motifs with which his imagination has
been obsessed sometimes for as long as decades.[2] The
author himself said that every novelist originally
wanted perhaps to write poetry and then, after failing,
turned to the short story and the novel: "I wanted to
be a poet, and I think of myself now as a failed poet,
not as a novelist at all but a failed poet who had to take
up what he could do," he ventured twenty-five years
after *A Green Bough* at the class conferences at the
University of Virginia.[3] In any case, that is the process
by which Faulkner developed.

As previously noted, *The Marble Faun*, Faulkner's
first book, was published in 1924 in Boston by The
Four Seas Company. The publication was arranged
and financed by Phil Stone. George P. Garrett, Jr.,
describes the work as an attempt:

to make a mythological poem, composed in a language of
echoes and innuendoes and arranged in a kind of musical
order. This was fixed in the formal context of traditional
conventions of the English eclogue, using the cycle of the
four seasons and the hours of the day to establish a relationship between separate poems. The effect gained by joining
the evocative method of symbolist poetry with the highly
developed patterns of the English pastoral is a unique con-
junction.[4]

Specifically, the book represents Faulkner's first
use of the mythological figure of the hermaphrodite,
which was to become a key figure in his work. The
phrases "slender girls" and "slender graceful feet" (in
the "Prologue") anticipate Patricia and Cecily. The
Faun and Pan point toward Januarius Jones and the
Rector.[5] "Nymphs troop down the glade":

> They near the marge, and there they meet
> Inverted selves stretched at their feet,

and then they slip into the pool that was their mirror.[6]

Certain scenes in *Mosquitoes*, certain figures and symbols, are anticipated here, still sketched with Greek backgrounds and Greek costumes. Swimming scenes are later removed from a classical setting and pictured more naturalistically in modern environments. When Phil Stone, in his preface, admitted that those first poems "have the defects of youth"—impatience, unsophistication, and immaturity—he also expressed his hope that the poet would progress and the belief that he showed promise:

It is inevitable that traces of apprenticeship should appear in a first book but a man who has real talent will grow, will leave these things behind, will finally bring forth a flower that could have grown in no garden but his own.

Nine years later, Faulkner had indeed matured poetically. *A Green Bough* is no longer simply an echo of mythological voices. The edition contains forty-four numbered poems. The opening is somewhat in the style of T. S. Eliot's *The Waste Land:*

We sit drinking tea
Beneath the lilacs on a summer afternoon.

In the novel *Pylon*, written a year after *A Green Bough*, the penultimate chapter is named after Eliot's poem "The Love Song of J. Alfred Prufrock." Generally, the influence of Faulkner's lyrical predecessors is obvious throughout. Faulkner, Phil Stone assured us in 1924, was "deeply schooled in the poets" and it "is inevitable that this book should bear traces of other poets," but the new volume gives the impression of being eclectic in principle. Quite abruptly, too, we

plunge into the world of e.e. cummings with no capi-
talization or punctuation:

> and let
> within the antiseptic atmosphere
> of russel square grown brisk and purified
> the ymca. . . .[7]

Baroque ideas of vanity and mortality prevail:

> Man comes, man goes, and leaves behind
> The bleaching bones that bore his lust. . . .[8]

They are congenial to the representative of a decaying
Southern culture, who also wrote of "the strife of flesh
that dies." [9]

Something of Robert Louis Stevenson's "Requiem" can be traced in the lines:

> The sun lies long upon the hills,
> The plowman slowly homeward wends.[10]

And, again, we find the nymph, the faun, and the
satyr of classical vocabularies, but in a more modern
and more mature version:

> It was a morning in late May:
> A white woman, a white wanton near a brake,
> A rising whiteness mirrored in a lake. . . .[11]

Poems I, V, X, and XLI ("Her unripe shallow
breast is green among / The windy bloom of drunken
apple trees") in particular might indicate that Faulkner,
even with traditional terms, was on his way toward
poetic originality. In 1933, however, the collection of
poems was already out of place between such epic
achievements as *Light in August* (1932) and *Pylon*
(1935), the novel that turned to a new theme, aviation.

Faulkner's tendency toward lyrical impressionism
and poetic expression continues to appear in all his

prose writings, constituting both his weakness and his strength. At the class conferences at the University of Virginia, Faulkner said:

It may be I've often thought that I wrote novels because I found I couldn't write the poetry, that maybe I wanted to be a poet, maybe I think of myself as a poet, and I failed at that, I couldn't write poetry, so I did the next best thing.[12]

Some lines toward the end of his late novel *The Mansion* seem to confirm his divided appreciation of himself; they suggest poetry rather than prose:

the ground already full of the folks that had the trouble but were free now, so that it was just the ground and the dirt that had to bother and worry and anguish with the passions and hopes and skeers, the justice and the injustice and the griefs, leaving the folks themselves easy now, all mixed and jumbled up comfortable and easy so wouldn't nobody even know or even care who was which any more, himself among them, equal to any, good as any, brave as any, being inextricable from, anonymous with all of them: the beautiful, the splendid, the proud and the brave, right up to the very top itself among the shining phantoms and dreams which are the milestones of the long human recording—Helen and the bishops, the kings and the unhomed angels, the scornful and graceless seraphim.[13]

Naturally, as "poetic" as this passage, or others, may be, it still does not fit even Faulkner's own definition of poetry. Asked, at the University of Virginia, about his definition of poetry, Faulkner answered: "It's some moving, passionate moment of the human condition distilled to its absolute essence." Exactly this "distilling" is the quality that Faulkner, whether writing poetry or prose, is most conspicuously lacking.

ooo

The Meaning
of Failure

After these varying attempts at finding both a style and a literary medium, Faulkner wrote his two masterly novels, *The Sound and the Fury* and *As I Lay Dying*. They are among the most fascinating and revealing pieces of modern American prose. Relatively thin volumes, they nevertheless—or therefore—contain something of the "essence" or even "absolute" essence that Faulkner demanded of poetry. Further, they contain many layers of reality that are not easily fathomed.

In 1945, Faulkner in *The Portable Faulkner* (published 1946) added an "Appendix" in which he traced once more the ancestry of the Compsons from the year 1699 to the end of World War II, and which was lacking in the original edition (1929). This appendix clarifies the chronology of events in *The Sound and the Fury*. In the beginning there is Ikkemotubbe, "a dispossessed American king," who:

granted out of his vast lost domain a solid square mile of virgin north Mississippi dirt as truly angled as the four corners of a cardtable top . . . to the grandson of a Scottish refugee who had lost his own birthright by casting his lot with a king who himself had been dispossessed.[1]

On this "square mile of virgin Mississippi dirt" the property of the Compsons is based, a proud possession on which their rise, the apex of their greatness, and their fall take place—the colonial period, the antebellum era and the Civil War—and of which, much later, after 1900, "the remaining piece of the old Compson mile . . . had been sold to pay for" Quentin III's "year at Harvard." [2]

Quentin III commits suicide in 1910. Also in that year the story of *The Sound and the Fury* begins, but not the book itself. The book begins on April 7, 1928; in the second chapter, Faulkner flashes back to the year 1910. Faulkner undoubtedly had his reasons for not relating his story chronologically; by rejecting the normative power of time, he gained something else—psychological depth and unique perspective. Thus, the first chapter is seen from the point of view of an idiot and from the most hidden and unreachable layers of consciousness; the last chapter from the "normal" point of view of a "realistically" thinking person. In this fashion Faulkner, through his arrangement of scenes, indicates the gradual succession of layers of consciousness and condemns—or accepts—the scale of values of civilization. The four chapters of the book bear the following dates: April 7, 1928—June 2, 1910 —April 6, 1928—April 8, 1928. We are warned, in this way, that we can look forward neither to a traditional "plot" nor to a conventionally composed "novel."

Dominating the book is Benjy, the idiot. Through his utter helplessness, he subjects the family to his service. Pity becomes its own victim. Where domination of and by the sick exists, even health is no longer health; in this universe of mere "sound" and of "fury" nothing, indeed, survives. Life itself is only a dream, only a disease leading toward death. Around Benjy the tragic fate of the Compsons circles; with Benjy it ends. In 1933, he is committed to the State Asylum at Jackson, Mississippi, after his family as such has ceased to exist.

The first scene is written from Benjy's point of view or rather, it is written in a distorted fashion as an idiot, with whom the author is practically identical, can have no "point" from which he may "view" the world. Thus, the beginning text is—without that later appendix and its descriptive biographies—almost unintelligible: "Through the fence, between the curling flower spaces, I could see them hitting." Only after

monologues set in italics and after a dialogue between
Mother and Uncle Maury does the reader slowly become aware of the idiot's position—"I"—in the devel-
oping and highly symbolic fable. The book opens with
Luster looking for "one of they balls" on the golf
course, and the significance of the ball symbols in the
face of Benjy's sex problems becomes oppressive. To
prevent him from jeopardizing the public, Benjy is
castrated.

Quentin's emasculation takes the form of suicide
before he is accused of the kidnapping of a little girl—
a sex crime that he has in fact not committed. This
accusation has a parallel in Quentin's mind: he suffers
from the idea of having committed incest with his
sister Caddy.

The survivors are Jason and Benjy, the two
youngest members of the family. Jason, the pragmatist,
dominates the scene. He survives, indeed, but in the
end he submits to a liaison with a dubious person and
thus he also comes to the dead end of infertility, of
"emasculation," and to the end of the history of a
family.

Benjy is thirty-three years old on April 8, 1928. It
is Easter. Good Friday, Holy Saturday, and Easter
Sunday conclude the tragedy. Perhaps, however,
Faulkner's novel is not a "tragedy" in the Greek sense of
the word but a parable taken from the world of
Christianity. The dating of the events is not accidental;
and beyond "fury" and "sound," beyond death and
decline, beyond disease and decay some hope at least
remains. Benjy, the youngest, the mere unreasonable
creature, more beastly than any beast, is castrated,
killed, crucified; in his deformity he takes upon himself the total suffering and misery of creation. Faulkner took up this theme again, quite consciously and

deliberately, in his late work *A Fable*. Here Christ walks on earth in the person of the little French corporal. Benjy, the idiot, the suffering, helpless, but God-created creature may, then, be regarded as the parable of Jesus reborn in the Deep South at the time of its fall.

Both the orthodox Christian, of course, and the orthodox literary critic will reject this meaning and the literary form that it takes with Faulkner. The pure aesthete will also protest. The neutral reader, if he should exist, must, however, accept Faulkner and must also subject himself to monologues and stream-of-consciousness constructions and expressionistic paraphrases set in italics—he must learn to read in the three dimensions of time, independent of our mechanical chronology.

Faulkner is interested only in the psychic penetration of his characters; he throws his light from behind the person as well as from in front so that the spectator receives it full in the face or is even blinded by it. For long stretches he shows only schemes, shadows of persons, as in the decaying white society in the Deep South. It is a macabre picture. Even the obscurity of certain passages of *The Sound and the Fury* is intentional.

The Negroes, however, retain their sharp contours and their natural vitality. They are portrayed most naturalistically. Dilsey, the old servant, attempts to keep the disintegrating house in order until she moves to her daughter in Memphis. Luster, fourteen years old, has accepted with infinite patience the heaviest burden: to take care of the idiot.

Faulkner, who always insisted on the principle that the South solve its Negro problem itself without interference from the North, knows the colored people best. He appreciates the Negro as he does any other human being, "loves" him in the double meaning of the phenomenon *love* that dialectically turns into jealousy and hate just as quickly as into self-destruction and self-sacrifice. He pictures Dilsey and Luster as radically truthful and impartial: Luster the lazy, the renitent, eager for cheap pleasures and lies. Luster, however, has a heart that the white man often does not seem to have (he has only glands). Dilsey, moreover, on Easter Sunday morning, takes feebleminded Benjy to the church of the "nigger," although Frony, her daughter, remarks, "I wish you wouldn't keep on bringing him to church, mammy. . . . Folks talkin." "Whut folks?" Dilsey asks. "I hears them," Frony answers. "And I knows whut kind of folks," Dilsey retorts. "Trash white folks. Dat's who it is. Thinks he aint good enough fer white church, but nigger church aint good enough fer him." "Dey talks, jes de same," Frony says. "Den you send um to me," Dilsey demands. "Tell um de good Lawd dont keer whether he smart er not. Dont nobody but white trash keer dat." [3]

Even into the life of the colored people the germ of arrogance and false pride has penetrated. Frony is quite "white" in her attitude, although quite black in her skin color. She has lost her self. She stands between the races, and this step away from her people is, of course, no step forward Rather, the no man's land between "nigger" and "white folks" has to be seen as a ditch closed on both sides; no party on either side will have anything to do with one who no longer knows where he belongs and who does not identify himself with any group.

The full emancipation of the Negro will not come about, according to Faulkner, by the Negro slowly and constantly moving in the direction of the white, but by the Negro standing on his own place freely and independently. Emancipation is no gradual process toward the one side or the other, but a principal step toward freedom. Frony moves into a dead end. Dilsey, however, remains true to herself and thus is already emancipated while Frony wavers. Luster, too, remains true to himself but he has those weaknesses that characterize "a white nigger" (Frony). Dilsey is actually neither black nor white; she only *happens* to be a Negress, her skin color is altogether accidental, and neither glands nor skin color, but the heart, determines the true nature of a human being.

Faulkner's early theme of the hermaphrodite here seems forgotten or neglected; or, Benjy, the idiot, the ugly, sexless because castrated, stands as its antipode. It must not be overlooked, however, that he too, like the hermaphrodite, stems from the same hidden root of nature that so often shows the strange desire for the unnatural, its own death.

Also subject to the law of humanism—Dilsey's humanism—which knows no differences between high and low, smart and stupid, is the novel written as a sequence, *As I Lay Dying.* Here, however, the tragic aspects are somewhat lessened and partly turned toward the grotesque. The theme is a limited one, but the dimensions that are opened are vast. Addie Bundren, mother of five children, wife of Anse, the farmer, dies. Her last wish was to be buried in the cemetery at Jefferson which, however, is farther away than any other. The family wants to fulfill her last wish, but it has to overcome unexpected hindrances in getting to Jefferson. The river swells, the ford is impassable, bridges are destroyed, the detour seems endless. After a week on the road the decaying corpse in the primitive, homemade coffin attracts buzzards. The coffin seems threatened with destruction by fire and water, but in the end it is laid in the ground. Thus, the elements work for the disposal of Addie Bundren. " 'Who the hell can't dig a damn hole in the ground?' Jewel says. 'It ain't respectful, talking that way about her grave,' Pa says." [4]

The family, too, fights with nature, matter, fate. Cash, the carpenter, breaks his leg. Darl must be taken to the lunatic asylum. Dewey Dell is pregnant, though unmarried, and on the way to the cemetery tries to procure from the druggist something to relieve her of her child—but is seduced again. Dust to dust, fruit to fruit: neither the dead person nor budding life can escape its destiny. Only Anse, the old man, who reckons with every penny and even digs the grave himself, *seems* to fight successfully the laws of nature; in the end he buys for himself a new set of teeth and gets married again, no longer fighting nature, but submitting to it. He is married to

a kind of duck-shaped woman all dressed up, with them kind of hard-looking pop eyes like she was daring ere a man to say nothing. . . . "It's Cash and Jewel and Vardaman and Dewey Dell," Pa says, kind of hangdog and proud, too, with his teeth and all, even if he wouldn't look at us. "Meet Mrs. Bundren," he says.[5]

This improbable tragic-grotesque story demanded a special form of writing. Out of more than fifty short sketches, each told by one person, Faulkner assembled a mosaic of psychological analyses. Besides the members of the family, various relatives, neighbors, and friends enrich the narrative with tales told from their point of view. The effects on the reader vary, touching his emotions or his sense of humor. This book is, perhaps, Faulkner's most congenial, most typical. In

Addie's monologues much of the author's own philosophy is reflected:

"He had a word, too. Love, he called it. But I had been used to words for a long time. I knew that that word was like the others: just a shape to fill a lack; that when the right time came, you wouldn't need a word for that any more than for pride or fear."

Faulkner seems to show here his own skepticism in regard to "the word," spoken or written; it is a form of literary skepticism revealed by any writer who is genuinely and dialectically bound to and repelled by the word. For all his eloquence and rhetorical style, a form of literary humility that borders on silence is immanent in Faulkner. Especially in his two most experimental novels, *The Sound and the Fury* and *As I Lay Dying*, he time and again suggests that writing, at least for him, is either writing creatively in new forms and avoiding clichés or not writing at all. At the same time and in the same vein, Faulkner suggests that human life, too, is more than a number of known words and that something transcending ratio and reason escapes the grasp of literature. He shares with Shakespeare, from whom the title *The Sound and the Fury* is taken, and with Hamlet the view that "there are more things in heaven and earth than are dreamt of in philosophy."

6

ooooooooooooooooooooooooooooooooooooooooooooooo

Money
and
Literature

Even *Sanctuary*, which was written purely to make money, does not conceal Faulkner's literary qualities. The author himself said of this novel:

Well, that book was basely conceived. I had written and had never made much money, and I—when I was footloose and I could do things to make money—I could run a bootlegging boat, I was a commercial airplane pilot—things like that—then I got married and I couldn't do things like that anymore, and so I thought I would make a little money writing a book. And I thought of the most horrific idea I could think of and wrote it. I sent it to the publishers, and he wrote me back and said, Good Lord, if we print this, we'll both be in jail. . . . So I forgot it, I wrote two more books, they were published, and then one day I got the galleys for *Sanctuary* and I read it and—probably it was because I didn't need money so badly then, but anyway I saw what a base thing it was in concept, what a shabby thing it was and so I wrote the publisher and he said, We can't do that because I've had plates made and that costs something. And I said, Well, I'll just have to rewrite it.[1]

In another context, Faulkner claims never to have lived among people who write fiction and not to have known that money could be earned with such books, but he knew such people indeed and he knew, too, that money could be earned that way; he did not simply "think of the most horrific idea" but only exaggerated certain events and features that were known to him, and in the end he wrote a book that is Faulkner, not at his worst, but somewhat distorted.

The story itself may offend the reader; but it is not the entire Faulkner. Temple Drake, another figure in Faulkner's series of hermaphrodites, is raped brutally and pervertedly, forced into a brothel, comes to like this situation in a way, is "saved" by her father and sent to, of all cities, Paris for the moral reconstruction of

tion. He must be regarded as an individual who bears characteristics of the type, and he is undoubtedly a type with a unique mode of behavior. In all his sense of being lost he keeps his dignity. He appears to be the highest and the lowest at once—a person who was born at the turn of the year at the time of Christ, a child without father or mother to care for him, but born in the hope of love, justice, and salvation.

At first Joe Christmas knows as little as the reader where he belongs. Is he black or white? A crossing of black and white? Is his skin different from any other skin known? Is he *only* an exception? Joe on the search for a self. He begins to move and to look. He has no relation as yet to his own self. His search is full of haste and convulsion. He searches for something that he is not sure exists at all. He has no base, no home from which to start, and does he have an end?

When he accepts a job, he accepts it under emotional protest. Without any special enthusiasm he makes something like a home near an old mansion where he might feel secure. He sleeps in a shack. He has an affair with the white owner of the mansion, Miss Burden, a combination of nymphomaniac and old maid and, again, a hermaphroditic type. Finally, he kills her (because she is, just like her name, a "burden" to him and herself). Joe Christmas is lynched. Only here, in the passion of hanging, does he find a self. In this crucifixion, in his own death, his life finds a climax. As with Benjy in *The Sound and the Fury* and with the corporal in *A Fable*, a modern version of martyrdom is offered.

The story around Joe Christmas is dialectically imbedded in the plot around Lena—Magdalena, the great sinner and penitent who gives birth to an illegitimate child above whom is the "light" (in August) of love and hope. In the end its fate may not differ greatly from that of the other illegitimate, Joe Christmas. Lena is, in contrast to Joe, the person who always knows who she is, wherever she may be, at home or on the road. Lena, in contrast again to Miss Burden's hermaphroditic homelessness in her own home, finds friends among strangers. In her motherhood Lena recognizes meaning and fulfillment; Miss Burden and Joe Christmas have no children and cannot experience this deep satisfaction. Lena follows her instincts while her consciousness is sleepy; Miss Burden and Joe Christmas despite their intelligence are lost creatures. The mother survives, whereas Joanna Burden dies horribly and Joe is emasculated. In Lena's body, in the center of her being, life continues; the brain and sex of the other two persons, bodily and existential extremes, must perish. "Motherhood" remains the lasting realm in which Heaven and Hell are only loose attributes. Finally, hermaphroditism appears as the form of nihilism that Faulkner has reserved for the useless.

One wonders how much religious tradition, how much mysticism has found its way into Faulkner. Apart from the rigorous and intolerant fundamentalism of a McEachern and the helpless confessionalism of a Reverend Hightower, Faulkner seems to believe in the practical-moral Christian who continues the mission of Jesus Christ. Beyond any orthodoxy, the laws of forgiveness and of love have to take on meaning. Already in Faulkner's early book *Soldiers' Pay* the rector makes certain anticlerical remarks. "We make our own heaven or hell in this world," he says. "Who knows; perhaps when we die we may not be required to go anywhere nor do anything at all. That would be heaven." [2]

Such passages may recall some words, or at least some ideas, of Jacob Boehme, the German mystic who even today has followers in parts of Pennsylvania. In any case, the sort of mysticism expressed by the rector represents Faulkner's striving for a synthesis or union of opposites. His idea of the hermaphrodite, too, is only part of a philosophy that describes contrasts which can be overcome. Whether the opposite are man and woman or, more generally, male and female, whether they are creator and creation, heaven and earth or heaven and hell, or whether they are—as in *Light in August*— Joe Christmas and Miss Burden on one side and Lena on the other: harmony can exist. Lena especially demonstrates that even in one person—here the center of the novel—a *unio fruitiva* of individual experiences can occur.

As antithetical as the persons is the construction of this important novel. Faulkner divided it into the two stories of Lena and of Joe Christmas, who personally never come into contact and whose only connection is Joe Brown. Brown is the former lover of Lena and father of her child. He betrays Lena as well as Joe and must accept the role of Judas. He avows neither the child nor the mother, and his relationship to Joe is, in the end, based on financial advantage: he wants to collect the reward that was offered for the arrest of the murderer. He loses everything, however, love and money, and proves to be a scoundrel besides being a Judas. Brown—cowardly, lazy, impertinent, stupid— has no stature at all, in contrast to Joe Christmas.

Between Brown and Lena, between Judas and Magdalena, stands Byron Bunch. On the one hand, he is characterized by helpfulness, genuine sympathy for the pregnant Lena, and the persistence with which he pursues his goal of marrying her; on the other hand, we must see in him a tragicomic figure in his doglike subjugation, half "Byron," the melancholy type, and half "bunch," one of the crowd and as undistinguished as man without a face. Bunch comes to visit Hightower (steeple of Christianity in an ironical perspective) in order to see his advice; Joe Christmas, too, comes to see Hightower and is murdered by the mob. Powerless, Hightower stands between the parties, self-indulgent and without much dignity. Hightower, dismissed pastor, whose Christianity has only by chance come to have an effect (as when he substitutes for a physician in the moment of childbirth), remains behind in the moral no-man's-land.

Reviews and flashbacks fill in the gaps in the history and background of these persons. Faulkner, however, is not always successful when he uses those modern literary methods; psychological discourses, especially on Joe Christmas, rather tend to blur the individual-symbolical contours than to sharpen them. Instead of myths—and Faulkner wants to create myths —we get only analyses; instead of James Joyce's Ulysses or Thomas Mann's Joseph (in whom myth and psychology, along Kerényi's lines, are united) we have only Sigmund Freud. The work of James Joyce and Thomas Mann, however—the two greatest writers of his time, as Faulkner himself attested—was precisely that which Faulkner attempted to surpass.

If we follow the contents of *Light in August* further without paying too much attention to the psychological network that Faulkner has spun around his plot, we penetrate through the fictional surface to archetypes of human behavior and to categories of life in general. We discover, for example, The Destroyer embodied in Joe Christmas, who kills not so much because he has, subconsciously, to kill but because he fulfills a mission that his victims prescribe for him. Those to be destroyed demand their destruction because they know they are failures and not strong enough to survive; they are the dead ends of nature. Such an ill-developed figure is the hermaphrodite Miss Burden who is a burden to herself, to Joe Christmas, and to life. She has neither the moral power to remain a virgin nor the libidinous courage to accept her role as Joe's mistress. Undecidedly she swerves between frigidity and ecstasy; the first annoys her, the other overwhelms her. She cannot make up her mind to bear a child, and she cannot abandon her desire and remain barren.

Because she is not strong enough to commit suicide, she provokes her own murder. Joe takes up the role of the garbageman, so to speak, of nature. Miss Burden—in the indecision that admits only one certainty: to have missed the real meaning of life—does not only allow and does not only suffer the murder; she demands it from Joe:

As he passed the bed he would look down at the floor beside it and it would seem to him that he could distinguish the prints of knees and he would jerk his eyes away as if it were death that they had looked at. . . . And as he sat in the shadows of the ruined garden on that August night three months later and heard the clock in the courthouse two miles away strike ten and then eleven, he believed with calm paradox that he was the volitionless servant of the fatality in which he believed that he did not believe. He was saying to himself *I had to do it* already in the past tense; *I had to do it. She said to herself.*[3]

The revolver that she points at him fails; his razor succeeds in the act that the woman demands of him.

Joe Christmas should be seen not only as Destroyer, however, but also as Liberator. With destruction, room is being made for new life; death is only a transit station. Joe himself, his kind, his name, perishes, and where hermaphroditic Miss Burden hindered the procreation of life, Lena will succeed in freeing life. Joe, himself powerless, clears the path so that the light in August may shine again. A person like him, who from his birth, from the beginning in an orphanage as a foundling, encountered only distrust and hate, must pay back with distrust and hate.

Love here does not precede but follows death. He had his first affair with a small-town waitress, who was half venal and half willing to be seduced. He had to knock her substitute father (McEachern) down in order to be with her; to do away with people or to destroy them is here, too, the condition for his love.

Joe Christmas is the same age as Benjy or the Corporal in *A Fable*—thirty-three—when he is lynched. Faulkner, so keen to tell the story of "Joseph Christmas," is consequently just as keen to remind the reader, symbolically, of Good Friday and Ascension Day. Christmas leads to Easter; birth and death and resurrection of life are the laws under which Joe *and* Lena exist, the couple that constitute the two aspects of this novel.

The writer as a frustrated theologian: this theme is a striking feature of Faulkner's complete work—or, taken another way: the theologian as a frustrated author of sex-and-crime thrillers. Faulkner manages to steer a course between too obvious religious symbolism on the one hand and too obvious cheap-novel style on the other, and if he succeeds, then he does so out of sheer literary mastery. In two books he strays slightly from this course—in the primitively constructed world of *Sanctuary* and in the too complex world of *A Fable*.

When he was not writing *Absalom, Absalom!*, he turned to attempts at a book that eventually came to bear the title *Pylon* (1935). This novel about a pilot is technically well done but lacks all the artistic virtues that makes *Light in August* a literary triumph. It apparently abounds in technical details of aviation without, however, being dull. On the contrary, it is one of Faulkner's most exciting plots. He spins his yarn; re-flections are kept to a minimum; a lively dialogue drives the story on. These qualities made it one of Faulkner's first international successes.

The setting is near New Orleans. The season: Mardi Gras. "New Valois" is the name of the town where new forms of courage are at work, new heroes, new knights in the leather armor of pilots. The pilots are befriended by reporters, and the reporter is the new troubadour of the new knights. Hero and singer are, as in other heroic ages, the necessary combination. The reporter does not remain a passive figure; he is drawn into the action of the narrative.

A special attraction of Mardi Gras is a stunt-flying contest. The pilot Roger Shumann flies inferior planes successfully until he crashes; accompanied by the para-chuter Jack Holmes, Jiggs the mechanic, and Laverne (with the little boy that maybe either Shumann's or Holmes's child). Money is always scarce. The reporter helps; without financial means himself, he knows from time to time how to procure a few dollars. Almost job-less, he tries to get Shumann a new plane. But Dean's fate (Faulkner's brother), Icarus's fate, Donald Mahon's fate, the last Sartoris's fate, become also Shumann's. All of Faulkner's experiences since World War I in the Royal Air Force in Canada (which had gone into stories like "Turnabout" or "All the Dead Pilots") are here collected and concentrated in the modern myth of the flier as symbol of a new age, symbol of twentieth-century attempts in the atmosphere and beyond.

Faulkner, however, also depicts the moral ambi-guity of technological advance, of a dubious form of mere technical and material progress. Laverne's love becomes deadly. The wife of the flier appears as both whore and mother, as lasciviousness and faithfulness; she has few scruples but at the same time cares infinitely. An orphan herself, she finally knows nothing better to do with the boy than to leave him to his grandparents. Motherhood, loyalty, and care break down in the face of bondage, sex, and lust. After Roger Shumann's death she follows the parachutist; he too, has already been warned like Roger, but he, too, will hardly die a normal, peaceful death.

When Laverne, in the mechanic's dress, repairs the plane she seems all masculine; but in this dress she is especially attractive to men. Parallel to the perversion of the deadly machine is her own deadly perversion. She dominates men but borders on frigidity with her adherence to sexual promiscuity. She represents the type of the completely "emancipated," modern, and in particular American, woman who, in gaining her emancipation and her freedom, has lost her genuine femininity and thus possibly her essential and real freedom—closely related to Faulkner's hermaphrodites of previous works since *Soldiers' Pay*. Since *Soldiers' Pay* Faulkner's imagination had certainly not lost touch, in its own peculiar "perverse" manner, with the border cases of double-faced womanhood.

The curse that hangs over Faulkner's people in the Deep South remains. Whereas *Light in August* somewhat weakens this curse and *Pylon* hides it in a too closely knit plot, it becomes more than obvious in *Absalom, Absalom!* (1936). Even the title makes this clear. The novel belongs to Faulkner's great literary period. The ill fate of the father-son conflict hangs over the Sutpens just as it hung over the house of David. In addition to hints of the Oedipus complex, the novel contains the fratricidal complex (both in the Civil War and in the family feud). Absalom, David's third son, had his half brother Amnon killed (Amnon had dishonored Thamar, their sister), escaped his father's revenge, and was later slain. In Faulkner's novel, Henry himself kills his half brother Charles Bon and in the end burns to death in the house of his father. Whereas *Light in August* shows parallels to the New Testament, *Absalom, Absalom!* is related, in its central theme, to the Old Testament.

The reason that Faulkner so often deliberately refers to biblical stories may in the last analysis be part of his upbringing in the Bible Belt of the Deep South— that region of fanatical, Protestant Church Christianity to which biblical speech and biblical archaisms belong just as much as religious intolerance and lynching. Faulkner's work portrays a long line of Protestant ministers, Episcopalians or Baptists, who have pledged themselves to two ideals: biblical teaching (as they understand it) and the traditions of the Deep South, love of the neighbor (as long as he is white) and dubious patrongage of the Negro, whether slave or so-called free (as long as he is no outright rebel). The harmony or conflict of the ideals is shown in the minister's special fate; the ministers' defense of incompatible values is the paradox of their own lives. This long line of ministers representing ambiguous sets of values begins as early as *Soldiers' Pay* and reaches to the minister of *A Fable*.

In *Absalom, Absalom!* we meet the representative of God in Mr. Coldfield, who in a first-rate symbolical gesture marries his daughter Ellen to Thomas Sutpen, a warrior, an officer of the Civil War who betrays Christian ideals (as limited as they may be) and especially the ideals of love and peace. Coldfield, however, as much as he may have subscribed to the Southern way of life, holds to his consequential pacifism: when the Civil War breaks out, he locks himself up, does not reappear, and dies in complete isolation.

Sutpen and Coldfield ruin themselves, each in his own way; the one by ambition, hate, and war, the other by self-denial, passion, and fanaticism. They are actually not quite so different; Sutpen goes into the Civil War out of brotherly love, and Coldfield's brotherly love leads to hate of all who do not do as he does. Extremes revert to their opposites, and the curse that seems to rest on the Deep South continues to hold sway over both warrior and priest, both Satan and God.

Thomas Sutpen, the hero, colonel of the Confederates, plantation owner, is cynically and scrupulously set on satisfying his lust for power and domination. He abandons his first wife and their son because he discovers Negro blood in his wife's family background. Seeking an heir to his possessions, he marries Ellen Coldfield, who gives birth to his son Henry, who disappears years later after the murder of his half brother. Sutpen then suggests to Ellen's sister, Rosa Coldfield (whose narration begins the novel), that they attempt to spawn a male heir; should this "attempt" be successful, he would be willing to marry her. Rosa refuses indignantly.

The decline of the family is certain when Milly Wash, granddaughter of a poor white, gives birth only to a girl, whose father is Sutpen. Milly's father kills Sutpen. Henry burns to death in the house. Quentin Compson, another narrator, commits suicide (as we know from *The Sound and the Fury*). Charles E. St. V. Bon, the Negro with the white skin, is a further representative of the sterile Popeye and Joe Christmas lines.

Even stronger than *The Sound and the Fury*, this

novel of fate is, in both its positive and its negative aspects, a stylistic tour de force in the grand manner. It is as violent as its people, as cruel as its material—the Civil War—and Faulkner, the artist, is equally brutal in his handling of the story. With stark force he formed the material that he later juxtaposed in interlocking episodes. Even his elegant rhetorical style does not weaken the harshness of the narrative. Chronology, explanation, and guidance are omitted; different layers of the narrative surmount or cross each other. Narrators other than Rosa Coldfield and Quentin Compson are allowed to speak. Each attempts to reconstruct the past and thus the "truth" in his own way. The results are both contradictory and complementary.

These different and differing points of view confront the reader like portions of a puzzle that he is called upon to solve for himself. Faulkner no longer takes the place of the omniscient author or creator of the story; the reader has to assist him as a co-author. A chart of persons and events will hardly guide him; instead, he should follow the plot as though on a tightrope that can be walked best, not by stopping now and then, but by reaching the end as rapidly as possible. The book should be read with the same breathlessness with which it is told, and only afterward should reflection take place.

Such advice on reading Faulkner has often been given by scholars, and it should actually be given again at every analysis. Faulkner's works are not to be understood by reading them line by line and word by word; they can most successfully be appreciated as a flow, and by active cooperation in reading. This is especially true of *Absalom, Absalom!*. Even the chronological and genealogical tables at the end of the novel will probably be more confusing than enlightening, because the novel is written not with, but *against* time, and *in spite of* the persons. The chronology and persons of *Absalom, Absalom!* are easily shattered. Faulkner offers only fragments and splinters. He moves through the ruins of the South like an archaeologist who is concerned about every find and who knows that if he misses even one piece he may be unable to reconstruct the whole. *Absalom, Absalom!* remained a torso.

The book belongs among the works of the late Faulkner and sets forth his principal motif—the decisive role that the Negro has to play in the ruins of the South. Charles E. St. V. Bon may still be only a suffering, passive figure, as Joe Christmas was; but he anticipates Lucas Beauchamp, who, at least, does something to save himself from lynching. He anticipates the "nun" Nancy, who actively enters life, and the Negro in *A Fable*, the bringer of salvation. "I think," says Shreve toward the end of *Absalom, Absalom!*, "that in time the Jim Bonds are going to conquer the western hemisphere." Faulkner, or Shreve, can have hardly meant this literally. Either it is supposed to be a sarcastic aside showing the Southern fear of being overwhelmed by the Negro or, more probably, it contains a moral message. In *Intruder in the Dust*, in any case, and in *Requiem for a Nun* this moral message appears specifically: here the Negroes—genuine Negroes and not white-skinned "Negroes" like Joe Christmas or Charles E. St. V. Bon—finally become the center of Faulkner's ethics.

7

○○○

*Novel
and Short
Story*

When *Absalom, Absalom!* was published in 1936, Faulkner was almost forty. Since his first book he had written about fifteen volumes, or almost one book a year since he came of age. The most mature works were written between thirty and forty, between 1929 and 1936. Within seven years he succeeded with his experimental writings like *The Sound and the Fury* and *As I Lay Dying*, with his attempt at commercialism (*Sanctuary*), and had finally composed the best novels of his early career, such as *Light in August* and *Absalom, Absalom!*. Intermediate works include *Sartoris*, *Pylon*, a volume of poetry, and some collections of short stories. In these seven fertile years he published a dozen books.

During the next two and a half decades of his career, a pause occurs in the late 1930's, and an ascent in the 1940's, with *The Hamlet* and then *Intruder in the Dust*. The climax of his intellectual endeavors and of his great epic works comes between 1950 and 1960: *A Fable* constitutes an attempt at metaphysics and religion; *The Mansion* is dedicated again to concrete human life. Scarcely a sign of fatigue appears in these last twenty-five years. Faulkner's literary vitality remained virtually unimpaired from his twentieth to his sixty-fifth year. *The Reivers* closes the human comedy that Faulkner undertook to portray.

Even the pause after *Absalom, Absalom!* was not an entirely empty one. Faulkner was occupied with a romantic escapade into the past and with several psychological experiments. The novel *The Unvanquished* (1938), built around the Sartoris family, is evidence of Faulkner's romanticism of that time. His talent for identifying his point of view with that of young people is demonstrated, again, in the vision of the Deep South through the eyes of a boy. All the Faulknerian traits—naiveté, pleasure in simple storytelling, humor, and optimism—are found in the saga of *The Unvanquished*, and will be found again in *Intruder in the Dust*, in the story about the boys who try to save Lucas Beauchamp from lynching. The world of infantilism, idiocy, premature sexuality, abnormal complexes, and juvenile morbidity that we know from some of Faulkner's previous books is put aside. *The Unvanquished* seems to be an attempt at introducing a new age free of racial intolerance and built by fresh, uninhibited young people without prejudice.

Thus Bayard, son of Colonel John Sartoris, grows up with Ringo, the colored boy, in the best of friendship and comradeship without, however, disregarding certain conventions. Ringo sleeps on a mattress on the floor next to Bayard's bed (but not in another room). Both boys and the grandmother remain on the plantation when the Colonel has gone to war for the Confederates. The uneven trio experiences the end of the war, defeat, the burning of the mansion, the loss of the Negro slaves, poverty, and famine. The grandmother dies at the hand of a robber. Sartoris returns safely, but is shot to death by a business competitor. Bayard, a member of a new generation, does not take revenge as may have been expected, but overcomes his opponent by disregard. He represents the "reconstructed" South in a new and positive way. The era of Colonel Sartoris is dead. Understanding and forgiveness are to follow hate and revenge. For Faulkner, despite his Davids and his Absaloms, the South has a chance to rejuvenate itself; like the phoenix, it can rise from the ashes.

Faulkner's optimism at that time, however, may not have been very profound; *The Unvanquished*, both the book and its persons, appear in a superficially romantic light. The composition of the novel is as conventional as its optimism. The episodes become adventure tales, and Southern romance is revived. Describing heroic deeds of the war, Faulkner seems not too far removed from Paul Bunyan. History is thus portrayed in the costumes of the Civil War; its uniforms seem to be taken from the local museum; the revolvers fire only when newly polished and repaired. The gunpowder smells as though it came from a Hollywood setting. The grandmother and her mule adventures in particular represent a retreat, as in a fairy tale, from reality into pure fantasy.

Only one year later Faulkner returns from the world of *Gone With the Wind* (preferred by Hollywood to *The Unvanquished*) to reality and the present age. Even here, however, Faulkner seems to confuse contemporaneity with modernity, and the phenomena of the 1930's with the timeless nature of man. Faulkner writes a historical novel of his own era. Even the addition of psychology helps him little. *The Wild Palms* (1939) is divided into two heterogeneous parts that cannot easily be read and understood as one piece (significantly, one part, "Old Man," has been televised without reference to the other part, "The Wild Palms"). The two parts or stories are, unfortunately, not printed separately one after the other, but alternate chapter after chapter.

The first story deals with two people who cannot come together despite their love for one another; the second with an escaped convict who risks his life during a flood in order to save a pregnant woman and in the end, has ten years added to his 190-year term. The two parts are combined at the end of the section called "The Wild Palms," when the young man, having been apprehended for accidentally killing his girlfriend, meets the convict of "Old Man." The theme that relates the two parts can be discovered in the attempted abortion in "The Wild Palms" and the saving of a pregnant woman in "Old Man." Birth—or the prevention of a birth—unites the two stories. The two couples are connected antithetically, as in *Light in August*.

Again, the question is posed: How do I act in the face of growing life? Cain was confronted with Abel, chaos with cosmos, decline and flood with creation and the end of the flood (as it was with Noah's Ark; Faulkner draws these parallels deliberately). In "The Wild Palms" catastrophe shatters an idyllic situation; in "Old Man" order reigns despite panic. The two stories, only loosely bound, generally lack depth. The first story returns to the bohemian life of New Orleans, as described before without much success; the other, the bucolic milieu of Mississippi that Faulkner pictures authentically but superficially. Lena and Joe Christmas remain figures in the reader's imagination, the convict and the woman of "Old Man" tend to disappear like shadows.

After these exercises at writing without great literary ambition, Faulkner definitely approached one of his major goals, beginning the trilogy *The Hamlet, The Town,* and *The Mansion.* In the final volume, *The Mansion,* Faulkner wrote:

This book is the final chapter of, and the summation of, a work conceived and begun in 1925. Since the author likes to believe, hopes that his entire life's work is a part of a living literature, and since "living" is motion, and "motion" is change and alteration and therefore the only alternative to motion is un-motion, stasis, death, there will be found discrepancies and contradictions in the thirty-four-year progress of this particular chronicle; the purpose of this note is simply to notify the reader that the author has already found more discrepancies and contradictions than he hopes the reader will.[1]

The Hamlet was published in 1940, about fifteen years after the basic conception of the trilogy. The rural scene of Mississippi prevails throughout in this American chronicle of three volumes comprising thirteen hundred pages. Faulkner's humor here breaks through with fundamental force. Faulkner, the early tragedian, developed into a master of comedy. Something of the spirit of a related author, of Knut Hamsun in his *Growth of the Soil*, can be detected. Again, we encounter the idiot—one of Faulkner's major types—who here has a love affair with a cow, and the madman who spreads death, the unfaithful, and the rascal.

The world has not changed radically since the early days, but Faulkner has become somewhat wiser and rests, for a moment, from his position as stern and rigorous judge of mankind. The fanaticism of his youth in its literary extremes as well as the stubbornness of old age lies far away. Full of mild sarcasm he reflects on the deceit and the cunning with which the Snopes and the Varners meet. They are families who, in contrast to the old-stock aristocratic though impoverished Compsons and Sartorises, represent the social climbers among the newer clans. The small, poor farmers supersede the snobbish feudal landowners. Instead of further explorations into the world of fame and misery of the Civil War, Faulkner turns to his own time and the future.

The Snopeses are quite "progressive"; to them, the ends justify the means. Mores and custom, tradition and old values are nothing to them. They are even suspected of arson. The people of the hamlet are determined to rid themselves of them as soon as possible. One Snopes, however, is more than two Varners. The Snopeses excel in cunning and unscrupulousness. They push the older residents like the Varners aside and surpass even the man who so far was reckoned to be the smartest in the county, the sewing-machine salesman Ratliff.

Faulkner here describes the South around 1890, one generation after the Civil War. The country is impoverished, decaying, but still relatively busy—not completely ruined by "The War between the States" and not yet fully infected by the striving for cars and industrial plants or the struggle between the classes. We enter an isolated hamlet on the edge of the mountains, in immense woods and dust; its people want to make a little money and many children. Politics is in the background. The historical halfway mark has been reached between the great battles of the old war and of the new war between classes, races, and political parties. The taking of ideological sides has not been forgotten, however; it has only been postponed and, in a way, anticipated. Eight years later it is executed, in *Intruder in the Dust*.

In his trilogy, particularly in the first two parts, Faulkner masters his material with great literary mastery. Despite all epic broadness, he—or his reader— rarely loses the story line as he did on many earlier occasions. Even where Faulkner has less space to develop his material, however, as in his short stories, he is entirely capable of condensing atmosphere, setting, a fate, without any loss of realistic detail. Unlike other writers of short stories before him, Faulkner seems most concerned with mastering a mood; the story itself develops as a result of that mood, and not the mood as a result of the story.

The best example, perhaps, for this perfection in grasping atmospheric truth can be found in "A Rose for Emily." In somewhat more than ten pages Faulkner succeeds in conveying the total mental climate of the Deep South through the reproduction of the surround-

ings of a single person. In the figure of Emily Grierson
an American fate is presented in its full ambiguity.
Once engaged, then deserted by her lover, she has become only half of that mythical Southern—or Northern—personality of an old maid. At her death the
mummy of her lover is found in her own dust-covered
house that was locked to any witness of the murder for
all those long years.

Behind these events, or rather behind this lack of
outer events, we observe Colonel Sartoris, the Civil
War, the invasion of the Yankees (her lover came from
the North), pride and past glory. The "divided house"
of which Abraham Lincoln spoke before the beginning
of the Civil War, "the house divided against itself," has
here once more become portentous and significant
reality. The North may have won the war, but it has
died of its own victory. The South may have lost the
war, but exactly this defeat is the straw on which it
hangs. The defeat is the disease that holds our attention
to such a degree that even death is removed into the far
distance.

Miss Emily Grierson has refused to pay taxes to the
community, and no power in the world will coerce her
to do so. Her stubbornness—a major feature of Faulkner's psychology of heroes—defeats any and all author-
ity. When her father dies, she refuses to have him
buried, with the remark that he did not die at all. After
three days she yields, but this yielding is an exception.
The Yankee enters town; people talk of a marriage (but
Emily has already procured arsenic for herself), until
the Yankee suddenly disappears because of difficulties
with Miss Emily's relations. When her cousins are gone,
the Yankee reappears: "A neighbor saw the Negro
man admit him at the kitchen door at dusk one evening.
And that was the last we saw of Homer Barron."

As stubborn as Miss Emily herself is the smell of a decaying body that prevails around the house. No one dares to inform her of the complaints of her neighbors. One night four men secretly sprinkle lime around her house to kill the bad odor. One or two weeks later the smell goes away. Miss Emily locks herself up. Forty years later she dies. The room "above stairs" in which no person had been in forty years is opened after her burial:

The violence of breaking down the door seemed to fill this room with pervading dust. A thin, acrid pall as of the tomb seemed to lie everywhere upon this room decked and furnished as for a bridal: upon the valance curtains of faded rose color, upon the rose-shaded lights, upon the dressing table, upon the delicate array of crystal and the man's toilet things backed with tarnished silver, silver so tarnished that the monogram was obscured. Among them lay a collar and tie, as if they had just been removed, which, lifted, left upon the surface a pale crescent in the dust. Upon a chair hung the suit, carefully folded; beneath it the two mute shoes and the discarded socks. The man himself lay in the bed. For a long while we just stood there, looking down at the profound and fleshless grin. The body had apparently once lain in the attitude of an embrace, but now the long sleep that outlasts love, that conquers even the grimace of love, had cuckolded him. What was left of him, rotted beneath what was left of the nightshirt, had become inextricable from the bed in which he lay; and upon him and upon the pillow beside him lay that even coating of the patient and biding dust. Then we noticed that in the second pillow was the indentation of a head. One of us lifted something from it, and leaning forward, that faint and invisible dust dry and acrid in the nostrils, we saw a long strand of iron-gray hair.[2]

Some of Faulkner's short stories or their themes reappear in his novels, as "The Hound" in *The Hamlet* or "That Evening Sun" in *Requiem for a Nun*. A motif as important as lynching is taken up, again, in "Dry September." Miss Minnie Cooper pretends that she was accosted by a Negro—"nigger" Will Mayes—and a lynching has most likely occurred. Faulkner leaves all that in uncertainty. He is satisfied with some hints and resigns himself to sketching the types of men involved. The reader can surmise the actual events from their talk and their behavior. In any case, that month of the "dry September," which gets on people's nerves after sixty-two rainless days, is part of the reason that the community acts as it does. The month is, and determines, fate. Climate thus becomes a dominating factor. Heat and drought suffice to turn latent suspicion into active hate, to make the pretense for hanging a Negro seem real; a touch of sadism is enough to turn a man into a murderer, and a hallucination leads to a conviction for rape.

A "rumor," says Faulkner in the beginning, "the story, whatever it was. . . . Something about Miss Minnie Cooper and a Negro . . . none of them . . . knew exactly what had happened." [3] One thing, however, is absolutely certain: the tension, which has built up for over two months, will explode. "The gods," as the story would have read in earlier days, demand a sacrifice. In the age of psychology, however, one only needs a barber shop in order to introduce a murder.

The atmosphere of such a shop—which is dominated, even in less exciting seasons of the year, by gossip, resentment, intrigue, scandal, and in which idle small-town folk satisfy their curiosity and their need for communication—its physical and emotional heat, the constantly stirring ceiling fan, the humid air, the evaporations, the hearsays and the rumors: all of this comes together one Saturday evening to transform a group of Babbitts, lazy but out for sensation, into a lynch mob.

The mob, however, finds no peace in the blood of an innocent person; it finds only the confirmation of its own original guilt and sin

A reverse situation, just as full of latent danger, prevails in "Delta Autumn." A colored girl with white skin—Faulkner's favorite characterization for a person without roots—has a child from a white man and attempts, unsuccessfully, to persuade her lover to marry her. Old McCaslin, resting at the center of the story, says: "Marry: a man in your own race. That's the only salvation for you—for a while yet, maybe a long while yet. We will have to wait. Marry a black man." Self-identification still involves such superficial characteristics as skin color; in the future, race barriers may be lifted so that man can find himself in freedom. The girl, however, has different convictions and already thinks more humanly: "Old man," she says, "have you lived so long and forgotten so much that you don't remember anything you ever knew or felt or even heard about love?" [4]

Such themes of contrast of old and young, of attitudes of "let's wait and see" and actual progress, of despair, forlornness, and of hope make up the richness of other stories, including some in the early volume *These 13* or *Idyll in the Desert* (both of 1931), and *Doctor Martino* (1934), or the later *Go Down Moses* (1942). In the *Collected Stories* (1950) Faulkner brings in the harvest of a lifetime of experiences caught in a language that here is relatively brief and concise and that reflects both grandeur and misery, past and present, of a region that carries its foremost dimension in its name: *Deep South.*

8

$\circ\circ\circ\circ\circ\circ\circ\circ\circ\circ\circ\circ\circ\circ\circ\circ\circ\circ\circ\circ\circ\circ\circ\circ\circ\circ\circ\circ\circ\circ\circ\circ\circ\circ\circ\circ\circ\circ\circ\circ\circ\circ\circ\circ\circ\circ\circ$

The Negro

The broad scale of Faulkner's epic works and his awareness of the problematic issues raised in the more compact novels of the 1930's are successfully combined in *Intruder in the Dust*, published in 1948. Here Faulkner handles his narrative power and dramatic plotting much more successfully than in such early works as *The Wild Palms* or in the following *Requiem for a Nun*. Clearly, prose alone does not necessarily make a good story and dialogue not necessarily a play.

In *Intruder in the Dust*, for the first time in Faulkner's work, a Negro is placed squarely in the center of the action that takes place in the South. This Negro is, in addition, a "pure" Negro in that both his parents are pure Negroes. Everyone knows him, and he shows pride in his race. Here no misunderstading can occur; here the skin color proves the genealogy, and no escape is possible. The hybrid position of a Joe Christmas has become a problem of the past. Lucas Beauchamp, therefore, is a "nigger." The combination of his name from elements of French and of the New Testament suggests his metaphysical and his socal origin. Lucas (Luke), the apostle, is supposed to have been the son of a Greek slave who was freed. That is exactly the position of Lucas Beauchamp—the ex-slave who values his freedom above all.

Suddenly, however, this old, proud, and independent Negro is accused of the murder of a white man and is arrested. The mob, again, threatens lynch justice. The basic situation resembles that of "Dry September"; according to "normal" behavior and tradition Lucas Beauchamp will not escape his fate. The relationship between white and black has changed over the years, however, statistically as well as in Faulkner's attitude.

Thus, according to Federal figures for 1931 (the year of publication of "Dry September" in *These 13*), twelve lynchings occurred in the United States (1930 had as many as twenty); in 1948 (the year of publication of *Intruder in the Dust*), officially only one. Especially obvious was the reduction of lynchings in Mississippi, which, until 1948, had ranked highest of all states, with 533 recorded lynchings in less than seventy years. Faulkner, by reflecting this decline in lynchings, suggests a change in the mentality of the Deep South. As he will frequently show, however, he is quite aware that human sadism can appear in different forms and that the absence of lynchings alone must not necessarily be considered a sign of absolute progress. A bullet in the back is equivalent to a lynching; and pistols have taken the place of the rope.

During those hours while Lucas Beauchamp— imprisoned, outwardly calm, but tense—is awaiting his fate, two boys, one white and one black, and an old maid are trying to find the truth of the matter. Lucas has asked for only one thing: that in the course of the investigation the grave of the victim be opened; he says that Lucas' pistol was not the one that fired the deadly shot. The grave of Vinson Gowrie, who was supposedly killed by Lucas, is opened. Instead of Vinson a different dead person is found. Vinson's brother is finally exposed as a double murderer, and Lucas Beauchamp goes free.

This review of the plot rather conceals than discloses the actual substance of this literary indictment of the so-called justice in the Deep South. Any analysis of Faulkner's plots, however, typically reveals many additional features of artistic significance. Indeed, despite the plot (and despite the author's sensationalism with another violent theme in *Sanctuary*), *Intruder in the Dust* was not written as a detective thriller at all, but as a psychological and moral study of man under duress.

Indeed, Faulkner's novel comes close to being a thesis on the inviolability of human dignity as exemplified by the most unsuitable and most thankless object—a "dirty nigger" from Dixie, a creature that stands even below the beasts, as far as "white trash" from the Deep South is concerned.

The novel was published one year after Sinclair Lewis' *Kingsblood Royal*, which had marked a new phase in the relationship between white and black, at least in the literary public. Some circles of socially aware people had once more been brought into contact with the "American dilemma," to use Gunnar Myrdal's term. Even Hollywood broke through the taboo against filming stories about Negroes. A series of such artistically acceptable and morally more or less honest motion pictures as *Home of the Brave*, *Pinky*, *Lost Boundaries*, and *No Way Out* was continued with the film version of Faulkner's novel in 1950, one year after he had been awarded the Nobel Prize for Literature.

Intruder in the Dust is one more proof of the old Faulkner who can hardly be copied, despite all imitators. The device that for Faulkner is a successfully utilized artistic trick is for a lesser artist only a mannerism. Reflections, flashbacks, interior monologues, italics —Faulkner combines all these literary devices in his own personal, often rhetorical, style that sometimes uses brackets from top to bottom of a page instead of the conventional punctuation. Perhaps his "impotence" at shaping clear-cut phrases—an art at which Hemingway was a master—corresponds to the "impotence" of the protagonist who, again like Joe Christmas, resembles the more or less fatalistic "hero" or martyr driven by events. Other persons accomplish the deed that the "real" hero does not do himself. Lucas Beauchamp remains the Negro who, deep within, has still something of the former slave; he does not use all the liberty at his disposal. Unlike Joe Christmas, however, he is interested in his own survival.

Because of the helpfulness of three white people Lucas Beauchamp is not lynched, but the story will not have a "happy end." Faulkner's style as a tragedian can be very subtle. His view of the tragedy of man centers on the substance of human existence, on man's essence, and not on the particular circumstances of a man in a certain specific situation. When Lucas is finally freed, he and the whites around him return to a state of being that from the beginning seemed fateful and disastrous. Only after the removal of the most primitive grievances, such as lynching, will the actual and fundamental problem be discovered—that of human communication. Until this point the problem had been to remove false differences—those of skin color and race; under the condition of legal equality, however, the problem will be to develop moral readiness to act as man to man. This is the true human dilemma.

In the beginning of *Intruder in the Dust,* the boy who is to save Lucas Beauchamp from lynching enters Lucas' home after falling into a creek while hunting rabbits. His clothes are dried; he is treated like a guest. The boy offers money as a compensation. Lucas asks: "What's that for?" and he "watched his palm turn over not flinging the coins but spurning them downward ringing onto the bare floor." Two other boys pick up the money and hand it to Charles. Lucas says: "Now go on and shoot your rabbit. . . . And stay out of that creek." [1]

The creek, however, as an image, is everywhere, and people fall into that creek again and again. The tragedy of man in Faulkner's work is not—as was the inherent danger from the start—a mere tragedy of

Mississippi, Alabama, Tennessee, Georgia; it is not a provincial, regional tragedy. Faulkner's sense of perspective raised him above his soil and above a literary cult of "the earth," which was dominant elsewhere in the decades of his greatest creative activity, primarily in the areas of Europe dominated by fascism and (from which even Hamsun was not free). In addition to social and psychological problems he was aware of tensions that result from the "nature" of man—or from the situation of man in nature.

Emily, white, having poisoned her lover; aviators in war and sailors in "Turnabout" who are not aware of their heroism, do not take themselves seriously, and achieve their proper greatness only in death; Lena, pregnant, innocent in all "guilt," following her beloved and returning home without him but with her child; Nancy, Negress, victim of her Negro lover; Lucas Beauchamp, who after being saved from lynching insists that he be given a receipt for the little money paid for his defense, which a "damn nigger" has no right to have (end of the novel and the beginning of a tragedy) —all of these figures live in a network of fatal relations woven beyond the realms of psyche and society.

Faulkner offers no metaphysics as such; but his world of the corrupt and corrupted body of man points toward that which makes this body succeed or fail. All of his plots show an order that has been brought mysteriously into disorder. The disorder of his world, however, may contain an order that cannot easily be explained by reason. Lucas Beauchamp leads a life that seems, in all its utter confusion, of a meaningful structure. The discipline that he displays always conflicts with threatening, hidden, and omnipresent chaos. According to Faulkner tragedy means order and disorder, essence and failure, a balanced universe and nihilism at once.

The whites hate Lucas Beauchamp because of his pride, he conflicts with his environment, is accused of murder, defends himself only fragmentarily, is helped half willingly and half not, a second murder occurs, a father must recognize his son as murderer of his other son—and in the end Lucas Beauchamp goes free, prouder and surrounded with greater hate than before, and any wrong that he does will precipitate his destruction. His every gesture will be quickly interpreted as a provocation. The tragedy that remains around Lucas Beauchamp—the tragedy that he himself *is*—has taken on form, continuance, and duration, leading to a persistent sense of his tragic fate.

That a modern tragedy can be written as a novel, or that a novel can be written from the point of view of tragedy, was demonstrated by Faulkner only a few years later in the weak but characteristic *Requiem for a Nun* (1951). The problem of Lucas Beauchamp remains. Whereas Lucas gains freedom, Nancy, the Negress, gains only suffering and passion. Whereas Lucas wants survival, Nancy wants only death.

Nancy functions as housekeeper for Mrs. Steven, the Temple Drake of *Sanctuary*. That novel described her rape, her stay in a brothel, and her rehabilitation in Paris—stations which, in the end, did not lead toward full moral success; *Requiem for a Nun* shows her marriage, adultery, and second moral breakdown (or the continuation of the first). In order to save Temple Drake from catastrophe, Nancy attempts to keep her away from immoral acts; when this fails, she strangles Temple's baby in order to prevent the final catastrophe of the two children remaining without home and mother.

Nancy is executed for infanticide. Was her sacrifice in vain? Only someone misunderstanding Faulkner —or Faulkner perhaps misunderstanding himself— could doubt it. Nancy as a former prostitute and morphine addict does not seem the type of girl to bring salvation; she does not come close to Gretchen, the innocent infanticide in *Faust*. Faulkner apparently completely lacks the understanding of the innocent woman necessary to write such a tragedy as Theodore Dreiser's *An American Tragedy*, which Faulkner did not esteem highly.[2] Faulkner expects too much of his readers when he asks them to accept this story of a "nun" uncritically and unironically, because whenever the mere plot outweighs the aesthetic form the book becomes little more than a scandalous piece of writing that, except for Faulkner's style, might well have been a purely commercial success.

Further, this literary concoction about a "nun" who has no cloister in which to seek refuge is offered as a mixture of narrative and play, satisfying neither prose critic nor theater audience. The dialogue is particularly weak, consisting primarily of sex pathology or of melodramatic confessions in monologue style. In *Sanctuary* Faulkner managed to rise above sensationalism; in *Requiem for a Nun* he fell below it, and except for some of the excellent prose interludes, this work must be deemed a failure.

Requiem for a Nun might, however, be considered a parody because Faulkner, at the age of fifty, was hardly at the end of his powers. In this sense he was unlike F. Scott Fitzgerald, who failed when he became famous; or Sinclair Lewis, who produced one book after another almost every year but with no literary ambition or progress; or Hemingway, who, some years later, was to shoot himself. The difference, too, be-

tween Thomas Wolfe, consuming himself in his utter
restlessness, and Faulkner, rooted deep in the South,
was obvious from their youth on.

Faulkner, moreover, did not belong among the ex-
patriates such as Ezra Pound or T. S. Eliot. More than
any other modern American he remained true to himself and his native conflicts. For that reason, perhaps,
the conflicts remained true to him; Faulkner's writings
form a great revolving stage in the center of which
stands man in his forlornness. Partly original, partly
hackneyed as in *Requiem for a Nun*, Faulkner seemed
fascinated all his life primarily by one thing: sexual or
original sin as it takes place in the South.

9

°°°

Ends

Long before *Intruder in the Dust*—in the first half of the 1940's, when Faulkner seemed to take a pause from writing—he slowly and painfully began a book that, according to his own plan, would crown his life's work. Even if nothing were known of Faulkner's activity in those years, a remark at the end of *A Fable* would reveal that he was already working on this novel in "December 1944," and that he worked in such places as Oxford, Mississippi, New York, and Princeton. The last date he gives is November 1953. The first copyright dates from 1950, the second from 1954, the year in which *A Fable* was published.

The background of all of this may be guessed from the physical appearance of the book. The violet cover contains three crosses, which are repeated on the title page and before each chapter. The preface gives certain conclusive hints: the "basic idea from which this book grew into its present form" stems from two persons in California; Faulkner read the "story of the hanged man and the bird" in *Look Away* by James Street; the "story of the stolen racehorse" ("Notes on a Horse-thief") was published in 1951 by Hodding Carter and Ben Wasson of the Levee Press, Greeville, Mississippi. In other words, the "development of several quite distinct plot elements," [1] which made *Light in August* a success, prevented *A Fable* from becoming a unified piece of prose.

The long middle part of *A Fable*, built around the stolen racehorse with three legs, seems extraneous to the whole. The animal symbol leads to such "totemistic" features as the snake, bull, and (Trojan) horse known from myths, religious literature and quasi-history. Faulkner emphasizes that the reader must recognize the "depth" of the story, as when he explains:

why Eve and the Snake and Mary and the Lamb and Ahab
and the Whale and Androcles and Balzac's African deserter,
and all the celestial zoology of horse and goat and swan and
bull, were the firmament of man's history instead of the
mere rubble of his past.[2]

That is one of two possible interpretations of the substance that Faulkner wishes to "indicate."

The other, more organic or inherent, is the story
of the Corporal who starts a mutiny, of a modern Christ.
The passion of Christ is retold in the fate of this
French soldier of World War I, born in the Levant. Opposite the Corporal stands the old General. Father and
son, God and man, Jehovah and Jesus thus confront one
another.

In addition to the Deep South as representative of
the new world, Faulkner takes France and the old
world as scenery for the drama around the eternally
"lost generation" of mankind. Faulkner knew Europe
only slightly, as the book shows; the European passages
are much weaker than the Mississippi pages, and the
combination of the two tends to be superficial or arti-
ficial or both. Questionable symbolism and synthesis
make an "ill-conceived" book, as one of the latest
studies in Faulknerian research points out.[3]

A French regiment mutinies shortly before an attack, and is withdrawn from the front; the thirteen men,
rebels and their leader, are imprisoned separately, and
the Corporal together with two others is executed by a
firing squad. Marthe and the General accompany this
passion of suffering and death. The implicit moral: If
Christ were to come again, he would be crucified just as
he was two thousand years ago. Nevertheless, only
Christ, then and now and ever, can save the world of
war, suffering, and decline, of devil and hell. Christ

must be crucified time and again so that man can be reminded of Him time and again.

A Fable has all the typical characteristics of a broad, personal confession, of the magnum opus. The question is whether Faulkner deliberately set out to write a work of old age and wisdom comparable to *Faust*. Despite all philosophical penetrations the novel lacks genuineness, freshness, and originality. If from all of Faulkner's works only *A Fable* remained, little would be known of the real William Faulkner; but if only *The Sound and the Fury* and *Light in August* or *Absalom, Absalom!* remained, all that is necessary would be known.

Here again, and for the last time, Faulkner plays upon the theme of the hermaphrodite. First, about the middle of *A Fable*, the General has a vision in which he sees the "hermaphrodite" between knight and bishop, among angels and saints and cherubim, yelping "in icy soundless tone against the fading zenith." [4] Other apparitions include figures from the history of Western civilization—those that have dominated the ages, physically or symbolically or both, in varying forms and to varying degrees. Then, toward the end, the Negro appears:

He was a Negro, of a complete and unrelieved black. He emerged with a sort of ballet-dancer elegance, not mincing, not foppish, not maidenly but rather at once masculine and girlish or perhaps better, epicene. [5]

The Negro displays features that either are common to both sexes or that prove him to be sexless. His name is Philip Manigault Beauchamp, and he is going to live in Chicago after the war as an undertaker. He likes "dead people." Perhaps Faulkner had him in mind as a symbol of death, of equalizing death that is beyond sex and procreation. In any case, he continues the line of hermaphrodites—ageless figures—which Faulkner used from the beginning as exponents of ideas that seem both obvious and mysterious and that embrace the ambiguity of man and universe.

After *A Fable*—this unsuccessful attempt at a comprehensive philosophical opus—Faulkner finished the more truly Southern and more typical Faulknerian epic that began with *The Hamlet*, concluding with the novels *The Town* and *The Mansion*, dedicated to Phil Stone ("He did half the laughing for thirty years"). The circle closes.

The Snopeses are back again. After passing the Varners, they take over Jefferson and finally Mississippi—in their own corrupt manner. Thus we have the bitter chronicle of the newly rich. The formerly poor white farmers have become politicians, land owners, and members of boards. The Snopes way (and Snopes sounds somewhat like "snobs") to get ahead is soon emulated in the town: its mayor, De Spain, wishes nothing more than an affair with Mrs. Snopes:

De Spain was creating, planning how to create, that office of power-plant superintendent which we didn't even know we didn't have, let alone needed, and then get Mr. Snopes into it.[6]

Events from *The Hamlet* recur in *The Town*. The relationship between man and woman has reached a conclusion: Flem Snopes is impotent, and pure libido is embodied in Eula Snopes. Flem, the social animal, chases money; Eula, the sexual animal, chases lust. Through his wife's affair with Mayor De Spain Flem achieves a sound economic position. Eula commits suicide; Flem continues to climb the social ladder. Whereas Eula lived her own real life, however, Flem figures only as a shadow of financial transactions.

The town, of course, enjoys Eula's affair and her simple, undiluted, uninhibited sexual desires, even though the townspeople put on the shocked faces of provincial moralists. The relation of the town to Flem is exactly the reverse; he is silently mocked as the deceived husband, whereas in business circles he becomes the honored member of society. Naturally such a "culture" or society, in which all values are inverted, makes man a schizophrenic cripple; at the same time, however, only this schizophrenia makes social survival possible at all. Faulkner makes the diagnosis without knowing the remedy (the remedy offered in *A Fable* was conventional enough). The other persons in *The Town*, Gavin and Charles Mallison, who together with Ratliff represent three successive generations and thus the continuity of plot and place, cannot cure the split personality of their time either. In fact, they fall victim to it. All that is left are the new cars, Jaguars; Varner, eighty years old; Ratliff still talkative; a Snopes who owns a chain of wholesale stores across various Southern states as far as Tennessee and Arkansas.

In *The Mansion* Faulkner concluded the epic of the Deep South; 1957 and 1959 are the dates that bring Faulkner's trilogy to an end. Only one book was published after the Snopes chronicle; this was *The Reivers* (1962)—"A Reminiscence," as Faulkner calls it. Here the author returned to characters created in earlier novels. It is a comedy of morals, set once more in Yoknapatawpha County and the whole Deep South. It must be considered a light, funny book "and an engagingly happy one; and it seems," says Michael Millgate in his exhaustive study:

an entirely appropriate final volume in that long row of novels and short-story collections which demonstrates, merely at a glance, the security of Faulkner's claim to major stature.[7]

In *Faulkner in the University* the author admits that the

Snopeses will destroy themselves . . . there's probably no tribe of Snopeses in Mississippi or anywhere else outside of my own apocrypha. They were simply an invention of mine to tell a story of man in his struggle. That I was not trying to say, This is the sort of folks we raise in my part of Mississippi at all. That they were simply overemphasized, burlesqued if you like, which is what Mr. Dickens spent a lot of his time doing, for a valid to him and to me reason, which was to tell a story in an amusing, dramatic, tragic, or comical way.[8]

10

ooooooooooooooooooooooooooooooooooooooooooooo

*Faulkner
and
Hemingway*

Faulkner's literary power and force of expression are certainly enormous, and perhaps greater than that of any other American writer of the first half of the 20th century, not excepting Hemingway, Thomas Wolfe, John Steinbeck, or Henry Miller. For Faulkner, writing was apparently a form of catharsis; something monomaniacally violent is attached to his artistic performance. It came out of a state of psychic intoxication, and, not coincidentally "King Alcohol" was at least as important in Faulkner's life and work as in that of Poe or Jack London, O'Neill or Hemingway. Social drinkers, moonshiners, rumrunners, prohibitionists and their opponents, hard drinkers, outright alcoholics, idiots born of a long line of addicts—such are many of the characters that appear in Faulkner's works, beginning with the drinking veterans in *Soldiers' Pay* and extending to Ratliff, who fetches his flask of corn whisky from his pocket.

In this respect Faulkner certainly resembles Hemingway. Further evidence of their relationship occurs in the genesis of *The Wild Palms*, as Edmond L. Volpe notes in *A Reader's Guide to William Faulkner*:

Faulkner may have had his contemporary, Ernest Hemingway, in mind. There are a number of interesting parallels between Charlotte and Harry's love affair in *The Wild Palms* and Catherine and Henry's in *A Farewell to Arms*. A number of settings that Faulkner chooses . . . seem arbitrary until they are compared with Hemingway's settings.[1]

Michael Millgate suggests that elements in *Sanctuary* seem "reminiscent of Hemingway" in their intentions, although they are very different from Hemingway "in manner."[2] Faulkner's own remarks on Hemingway in *Faulkner in the University* prove that he was always quite aware at least of the "method" that Hemingway developed, if not of his writing as a whole as counter-point to his own. They both have a common "teacher" in Sherwood Anderson, who was born in 1876, well over twenty years before them, and whom Heming-way met in Chicago in 1920, and Faulkner in New Orleans in 1925. Sherwood Anderson thus stands at the beginning of modern American literature through his person and his work.

Like Hemingway, Faulkner went through differ-ent positions and held different jobs besides writing, al-ways searching for his own personal and legitimate means of expression. They both worked as newspaper reporters and went, in a typically American way, through the hard school of writing of the people and for the people. They both later described the reporter's job with great skill, fondness, and authenticity. As noted earlier, the New Orleans *Times-Picayune* was the first publication to print a story by Faulkner.

Although Faulkner and Hemingway were close in age (Faulkner was born on September 25, 1897, and Hemingway on July 21, 1899) and although they both represented the "lost generation," they nevertheless moved farther apart from one another than from any other major contemporary American novelist. Their styles differ in the same way that the Deep South with its lush vegetation, animal life, and forms of human existence differs from the rigidity of the North from which Hemingway developed: Faulkner shows ingen-ious bombast; Hemingway ingenious discipline. They were both stirred by Europe, World War I, and the disillusion of the postwar years. Their pathos is deter-mined by World War I and by the civil wars, Amer-ican or Spanish. General Stonewall Jackson, for exam-ple, is the hero of both.

In the 1920's both writers experimented with

poetry and the short story; in the 1930's they found
their individual forms of expression; in the 1940's they
extended their powers; and in the 1950's they reached
the peak of their development. The Nobel Prize for
Literature, given to Faulkner in 1949 and to Hemingway in 1954 (it could have been given in reverse order
or even simultaneously), superficially crowns the
career of each. Hemingway shot himself on July 2,
1961, Faulkner died peacefully on July 6, 1962.

The differences in their manner and temperament
have already been suggested. Their perspectives also
differed essentially, especially as far as literary traditions are concerned:

Indeed, it would seem fair to say that in certain important
respects Faulkner was more actively aware of American
and European literary traditions than any other important
American novelist of this century, Hemingway not excluded.[3]

Hemingway seemed to have rejected more or less
all traditions, as compared with Faulkner. The man from
the Deep South is foremost a searcher of souls, like the
great French, English, or Russian writers he admired
(Balzac, Dickens, Tolstoy, Gogol), and he follows
much of Freud in his analyses of sexual perversions. Detail, local color, locale, as authentic as they are, seem in
general mere pretexts, requisites, causes, and means for
inspiration toward the creation of psychic portraits.
Finally even the skin—sometimes almost literally—is
taken off the body under scrutiny in order to investigate
soul and body, flesh and blood, the first principal causes,
the archaic, the chthonic.

Surface exists in order to be penetrated. Faulkner's
style correspondingly involves digging, excavating, a
sort of archaeological style that endeavors to free man

from the historical and prehistorical layers that threaten to bury him. The style is breathless, indeed long-winded, sometimes confused and confusing; cascades of adjectives drown the figures on which they splash.

Faulkner's formlessness serves the one purpose of finding "form": a seamless presentation of the deepest human conflicts. His novels therefore are actually without beginning or end; *Absalom, Absalom!*, one of the most personal, direct, and typical of Faulkner's works, begins with a leap into Miss Coldfield's room, into the office, and into speech: "Her voice would not cease, it would just vanish." It ends as abruptly with the exclamation: "*I dont. I dont! I dont hate it! I dont hate it!*" These novels seem eager to continue life itself and are continued later by life itself: fragments, rhetorical interruptions of life's flow, immense and unbroken rocks, jungles of words, swamps of sentences, spasms, tropical storms.

Hemingway on the other hand seems foremost something like a behaviorist, a discerning scholar among writers when contrasted with Faulkner. His secret interests are sociological analyses, and their results must be "scientifically" exact and correct. He is fascinated by surface, fond of details as a seeming end in themselves; he draws sharp contours and an accurately observed milieu. His style must therefore be precise, and his technique (Faulkner would say "method") becomes almost transparent. Hemingway easily leads his reader to assume that he, the reader, can also write a story as "simple" and as short as "The Killers," in contrast to Faulkner, who suggests that he alone is capable of writing as "difficult" and as long a story as "The Bear" and that he is unique (and therefore is rarely copied, unlike Hemingway, who has many imitators).

Hemingway is precise and exclusive like a photograph. In his expression he prefers the hard blows and the direct aim at the target, like a boxer; he is concise like a searching reporter in contrast to Faulkner's reporter in *Pylon* who, unable to find the suitable word, says either none or too many. Hemingway's diction looks like a schoolmaster's example of lucidity. Telegrams can hardly be clearer and more to the point. With Hemingway, we review our old patterns of grammar: subject, object, predicate. Adjectives are his enemies and are for the most part deleted. Hemingway's novels always pretend to be objective and realistic, or are classified as such by literary historians; even if told in the first person, objective limitation is used.

Hemingway must be considered a true master of the short story characterized by its plot and action, whereas Faulkner's short stories rely more on their atmosphere. Nevertheless, Hemingway's short stories produce a cumulative sense of atmosphere, which becomes apparent at the conclusion of the plot. Faulkner writes in the reverse manner; his atmosphere generates a plot at the end of his narrative. Faulkner's persons talk and reveal themselves through and by talk; Hemingway's limit themselves to an absolute minimum of words. Faulkner produces a flood of words even if the story is short; Hemingway seems to use fewer words even in a long story. Hemingway's art, or his setting, therefore seems Spartan and stoic, and Faulkner's more Athenian and epicurean. Hemingway's works are cut out; Faulkner's flow over.

Both writers may have a common subject—man ("No man is an island"—Hemingway's motto taken from John Donne for *For Whom the Bell Tolls*), but their approaches to man diverge from the beginning: Hemingway goes around man, Faulkner through him.

On his detour on the round surface of man's earth (or "Continent," as John Donne said), Hemingway of course reaches his goal as surely as Faulkner, whose way is shorter but perhaps more difficult. Hemingway uses a network of global longitudes and latitudes, mathematical patterns laid over the landscape, while Faulkner mines far below the surface. Hemingway's surface is geometrically laid out so that he cannot miss his final objective; Faulkner's abyss is so deep that it opens on the other side of his globe.

Hemingway's "depth" must be measured by the length from beginning to end on a surface that can be surveyed; Faulkner's "length" must be measured by the depth underground that no man can fully appreciate. Hemingway is broader because he covers a wider variety of material and locales; Faulkner, however, is deeper. Who is "significant" or more "important" cannot be ascertained unless one side votes for Hemingway's expansiveness (he has more "world" in his work —the United States, Cuba, Italy, Spain, France) and the other for Faulkner's weight (a greater local density).

Hemingway has only one perspective, his own, which he carefully hides behind his persons. Faulkner has none, and each of his figures speaks the way he does and does not. With Hemingway only one truth of the story emerges from the interplay of all persons involved; Faulkner knows forms of truth, because each character tells his own version of it. From the separate perspectives of the speakers in *Absalom, Absalom!* or from the more than fifty points of view in *As I Lay Dying* we learn the contradictions of the world or of the contradictory world.

Hemingway always remains the "author"—the invisible creator, the maker of things; Faulkner appears himself, but we have no harmonious picture. Heming-

way remains Hemingway; Faulkner transforms himself
constantly without renouncing himself. Hemingway's
men therefore, and naturally his women also, remain
themselves, man as man and woman as woman, and
their sex is certainly determined once and for all;
Faulkner's figures often remain ambiguous, and one of
Faulkner's aims is to let a girl look masculine, a man—
like Flem Snopes—be impotent, to remove the precise
differentiations between the sexes, and to produce a
symbol of the first order—the always changing, always
transforming figure of the hermaphrodite. Each of
Faulkner's figures is his—or her—own author; they
show a masculine or feminine side as required in a certain situation, and Faulkner often has difficulty in keeping them within the framework of his plot. These
figures run away with and from him, and thus, as in
The Wild Palms or *A Fable*, the separate parts do not
combine properly, producing a divergence in form that
parallels the division in content.

Hemingway offers a single, clear reflection of
reality as he sees it and as we at once recognize it;
Faulkner offers a somewhat distorted picture of reality
that excels by its richness of contradictions, and the
reader has to look several times to recognize something
real at all. Hemingway's work is a creation in itself;
Faulkner's work is *his*, Faulkner's creation, exhausting
and exhaustive, approaching by some measure a form of
nihilism that has nothing to do with moral or existential, but with artistic nihilism. Unlike Hemingway,
Faulkner has no a priori literary form that is appropriate to a story (Hemingway's stories fit the characteristic form once developed and are somehow interchange-
able); with Faulkner, the content, the meaning, the essence takes on, if at all, a shape that comes from within:

slowly, while talking—and almost always a narrator talks—something like a literary structure develops.

On the first pages of a book Faulkner, like his reader, seems scarcely to know where he is going, and on the last page he seems just as surprised at the outcome as his reader. Certainly this turn of events is relative only to Faulkner's "knowledge" of the plot; his material comes from sources other than pure knowing, from the richness of his conscious and subconscious experiences, from the depth of life, from a wide memory, from far-reaching family traditions, from the storytelling of the old people who are always to be seen on the front porches of the white mansions or the shacks of the Deep South, or at the store or in front of the town hall—from the unique folklore of a whole region. Faulkner's story resembles lava that flows out hot and only slowly cools to shape; he is the writer as volcano, erupting at times with original force.

Faulkner, then, with his chaotic and creative approach to writing is as "hard" to read as Hemingway is "easy." Faulkner, moreover, like Hemingway, fools his readers. In the end he reveals himself to a careful reader just as Hemingway conceals himself in spite of careful reading. Faulkner's symbolism becomes progressively clearer; Hemingway's, however, is not always translucent. Thus to call one "complicated" and the other "naïve" because one is a difficult author and the other an easy one—or vice versa to call one "superficial" despite his depth because he uninhibitedly offers us his symbolism directly, and to call the other "deep" despite his interest in the surface because he knows how to decorate his symbols more skillfully—would mean to misunderstand them both profoundly. Faulkner is as true a "poet" as Hemingway is; both know how to reveal and to camouflage, and both succeed in showing man in ways that finally converge.

The "Gothic" novel of Faulkner with all its exorbitant and boundless dimensions, the "baroque" pomposity hiding order and ratio, the "Romantic" achievement of creating fear and desire—all these "anticlassical" criteria of the work of William Faulkner seem to find identity with the geographical setting of the Deep South in which the writer and his material originated. The hermaphrodite as one of Faulkner's major, though perhaps somewhat hidden, themes indicates the author's principal concern: to show that, contrary to the classical and thus typical experiences of our bisexual universe, a constant possibility exists for the synthesis of male and female within a single person, even on the basis of perversion; or vice versa, that perversion, tragedy, and the seemingly supernatural are only another means of achieving the natural. Our sexually divided world seems to seek, with Faulkner, that paradisiacal, prehistorical, mythical unity of existence and harmony of peace that is obstructed by both masculinity and femininity and that is attained only in the synthesis and abolition of sex. Because sex guarantees human mobility, however, we always fall back on and cannot live without original sin.

The state of utter intoxication that prevails in such natural-unnatural forms of life, as created by Faulkner, clearly differentiates his work from the utterly rational and classical sobriety that dominates Hemingway's literary cosmos. The unusual realm of Faulkner is exhibited most strongly in the calling up of elemental powers: of fear and longing, hate and wrath, charity and rape, murder and incest, sex crimes and lust for sex, pride and humility, death wish and libido, lust for death and longing for love. Here, archaically, "demons" are at work. Pagan gods, Eros and Thanatos, and Christian symbols like blood and body, wine and bread cross each other. We observe phallus and the crown of thorns, Hermes and Aphrodite or Hermaphrodite and Christ.

Faulkner, however, is as much modern man as Hemingway, and he also knows something about economics; in addition to the power of love the power of hunger exists, and both together govern the world. Money is the power that controls us from the outside, and procreation from within, but if the latter were not stronger than the former, mankind would have long since perished.

Faulkner knew the great writers of the Elizabethan Age and, in his poetry, he has copied some of them. He is at home in a world where motivations like those of Macbeth, Richard III, and Othello are well known; his South is shaken by the fever of passion, war, revenge, and forgiveness. The passions and their people (not vice versa) seem to be stronger than reason; the tilling of the soil that sustains them seems more lasting than the metropolis. Race conflicts are not conditioned only by socioeconomic causes; *smell* seems as important as class struggle. Faulkner, no doubt, belongs to the tradition of Dostoevski, Hamsun, Giono, Gerhart Hauptmann, to name only a few kindred spirits, rather than to that of Cervantes, Voltaire, Swift, or Thomas Mann. Faulkner's Joe Christmas is related to Raskolnikov and August, the tramp, from Hamsun or a dramatic character from the early works of European naturalism, and not to those men of irony like Don Quixote, Candide, Gulliver, or Hans Castorp.

Faulkner's persons, in conflict with themselves, mirror the human dilemma between good and evil. Faulkner's South is a symbol of that. The end of the novel *Absalom, Absalom!* indicates how difficult a single decision may be for man, and it does so in

Faulkner's characteristic manner. Shreve says: "Now I want you to tell me just one thing more. Why do you hate the South?"

"I dont hate it," Quentin said, quickly, at once, immediately; "I dont hate it," he said. *I dont hate it* he thought, panting in the cold air, the iron New England dark; *I dont. I dont! I dont hate it! I dont hate it!*

ooo

Notes

1. *Introduction to Certain Problems*

    [1] *A Green Bough*, poem XLIV, in *The Marble Faun and A Green Bough* (New York: Random House, 1965), p. 67.
    [2] *The Town* (New York: Random House, 1957), p. 50.
    [3] *Soldiers' Pay* (New York: Liveright Publishing Corporation, 1926), p. 67.
    [4] *Faulkner in the University*, F. L. Gwynn and J. L. Blotner, eds. (Charlottesville, Va.: The University of Virginia Press, 1959), p. 74.

2. *A Lost Generation*

    [1] *Faulkner's County*, Nobel Prize Address (London: Chatto and Windus, 1955), pp. vii–viii.
    [2] *Mosquitoes* (New York: Horace Liveright, 1927), pp. 144–145.
    [3] *Faulkner in the University*, p. 285.
    [4] *Sanctuary* (New York: The Modern Library, 1932), p. v.

[5] *The Mansion* (New York: Random House, 1959), pp. 428–429, 435.

[6] Michael Millgate, *The Achievement of William Faulkner* (London: Constable, 1966), p. 56.

3. *The Hermaphrodite*

[1] *The Sound and the Fury* (New York: Random House, 1946), pp. 9–10.

[2] *Soldiers' Pay*, pp. 99, 286.

[3] *Intruder in the Dust* (New York: Random House, 1948), pp. 238–239.

[4] Sigmund Freud, *Gesammelte Werke* (London: Imago Publ. Co., Ltd., 1949), Vol. 5, pp. 40–41.

[5] Millgate, *op. cit.*, pp. 16, 300.

[6] *Mosquitoes*, p. 252.

[7] *Ibid.*

[8] *Ibid.*, pp. 139, 147.

[9] *Sartoris* (New York: Harcourt, Brace and Company, 1951), pp. 373, 415.

[10] Irving Malin, *William Faulkner* (Stanford, Calif.: Stanford University Press, 1957), p. 46.

4. *Poetic Experiments*

[1] *Mosquitoes*, pp. 63–64.

[2] Hans Hennecke, *Ein grüner Zweig* (Stuttgart, 1957).

[3] *Faulkner in the University*, p. 22.

[4] George P. Garrett, Jr., "An Examination of the Poetry of William Faulkner," *Princeton University Library Chronicle*, Faulkner Number, p. 125.

[5] *Ibid.*, pp. 22, 38.

[6] *Ibid.*, p. 26.

[7] *Ibid.*, p. 20.

8 *Ibid.*, p. 24.
9 *Ibid.*, p. 26.
10 *Ibid.*, p. 29.
11 *Ibid.*, p. 8.
12 *Faulkner in the University*, p. 4.
13 *The Mansion*, pp. 435–436.

5. *The Meaning of Failure*

1 *The Sound and the Fury*, p. 3.
2 *Ibid.*, p. 10.
3 *Ibid.*, p. 306.
4 *As I Lay Dying* (New York: Random House, 1946), p. 506.
5 *Ibid.*, pp. 531–532.

6. *Money and Literature*

1 *Faulkner in the University*, p. 91.
2 *Soldiers' Pay*, p. 317.
3 *Light in August* (New York: Random House, 1932), pp. 263–264.

7. *Novel and Short Story*

1 *The Mansion*, Preface.
2 "A Rose for Emily" in *Collected Stories of William Faulkner* (New York: Random House, 1950), pp. 129–130.
3 "Dry September" in *Collected Stories*, p. 169.
4 "Delta Autumn" in *Go Down, Moses* (New York: Random House, 1942), p. 363.

8.   *The Negro*

[1] *Intruder in the Dust*, pp. 15–16.
[2] *Faulkner in the University*, pp. 233–234.

9.   *Ends*

[1] Millgate, *op. cit.*, p. 230.
[2] *A Fable* (New York: Random House, 1954), p. 161.
[3] Millgate, *op. cit.*, p. 234.
[4] *Ibid.*, p. 242.
[5] *Ibid.*, p. 374.
[6] *The Town* (New York: Random House, 1957), p. 15.
[7] Millgate, *op. cit.*, p. 258.
[8] *Faulkner in the University*, p. 282.

10.   *Faulkner and Hemingway*

[1] Edmond L. Volpe, *A Reader's Guide to William Faulkner* (London: Thames and Hudson, 1964), p. 214.
[2] Millgate, *op. cit.*, p. 121.
[3] *Ibid.*, p. 288.

○○

Chronology

1897: William Faulkner born in New Albany, Mississippi.
1900: Thomas Wolfe born.
1902: The Faulkners move to Oxford, Mississippi.
1914: Friendship with Phil Stone.
1918: In Royal Canadian Air Force.
1919: First attempts at writing. First publication.
1920: Trip to New York.
1922: Postmaster in Oxford.
1924: *The Marble Faun.*
1925: In New Orleans. Friendship with Sherwood Anderson (b. 1876). Publications in New Orleans *Times-Picayune.* Trip to Europe.
1926: *Soldiers' Pay.*
1927: *Mosquitoes.*
1929: *Sartoris. The Sound and the Fury.* Marriage.
1930: *As I Lay Dying.*
1931: *Sanctuary.* Faulkner buys mansion, built in 1840, in Oxford.
1932: *Light in August.* Trip to Hollywood.
1935: Faulkner's brother Dean dies in airplane crash. *Pylon.*
1936: *Absalom, Absalom!*

1938:   *The Unvanquished.*

1939:   *The Wild Palms.* Important critical appreciations of Faulkner's works (O'Donnell, Beck, Aiken, Warren). First prize of the O. Henry Memorial Award for short stories.

1940:   *The Hamlet.* Another first prize of the O. Henry Memorial Award.

1942:   *Go Down, Moses.*

1948:   *Intruder in the Dust.*

1949:   *Knight's Gambit. Intruder in the Dust* filmed in Oxford.

1950:   *Collected Stories.* Nobel Prize for Literature (for 1949).

1951:   *Requiem for a Nun.* "Notes on a Horsethief" (later part of *A Fable*). Elected member of the French Legion of Honor.

1952:   New edition of the novel *The White Rose of Memphis*, first published in 1880 by Colonel William Falkner, William Faulkner's great-grandfather.

1954:   *A Fable.* Pulitzer Prize to Faulkner. Nobel Prize for Literature to Hemingway.

1955:   Trip to Japan.

1957:   *The Town.*

1959:   *Faulkner in the University. The Mansion.*

1961:   Death of Hemingway.

1962:   *The Reivers.* Death of William Faulkner.

ooo

Bibliography

Works by William Faulkner

The Marble Faun (poetry), 1924
Soldiers' Pay (novel), 1926
Mosquitoes (novel), 1927
Sartoris (novel), 1929
The Sound and the Fury (novel), 1929
As I Lay Dying (novel), 1930
Sanctuary (novel), 1931
These Thirteen (short stories), 1931
Salmagundi (essays and poetry), 1932
Light in August (novel), 1932
A Green Bough (poetry), 1933
Doctor Martino, and Other Stories, 1934
Pylon (novel), 1935
Absalom, Absalom! (novel), 1936
The Unvanquished (novel), 1936
The Wild Palms (novel), 1939
The Hamlet (novel), 1940
Go Down, Moses, and Other Stories, 1942
The Portable Faulkner, 1946
Intruder in the Dust (novel), 1948
Collected Stories, 1950

Requiem for a Nun (novel and drama), 1951
A Fable (novel), 1954
The Faulkner Reader, 1954
Big Woods (short stories), 1955
Faulkner at Nagano (interviews), 1956
The Town (novel), 1957
New Orleans Sketches, 1958
The Mansion (novel), 1959
Faulkner in the University (interviews), 1959
The Reivers (novel), 1962
Early Prose and Poetry, 1962
Essays, Speeches and Public Letters, 1966
Lion in the Garden (interviews), 1968

Works about William Faulkner

Coughlan, Robert. *The Private World of William Faulkner*.
    1953
Hoffman, Frederick J. *William Faulkner*. 1961
Howe, Irving. *William Faulkner*. 1952
Malin, Irwin. *William Faulkner*. 1957
Millgate, Michael. *The Achievement of William Faulkner*.
    1966
Miner, Ward L. *The World of William Faulkner*. 1952
Robb, Mary C. *William Faulkner*. 1957
Van O'Connor, William. *The Tangled Fire of William
    Faulkner*. 1954
Vickery, Olga W. *The Novels of William Faulkner*. 1959
Volpe, Edmond L. *A Reader's Guide to William Faulkner*.
    1964
Waggoner, Hyatt H. *William Faulkner*. 1959